DAUGHTER,

THERE IS MORE TO YOU THAN MEETS THE EYE...

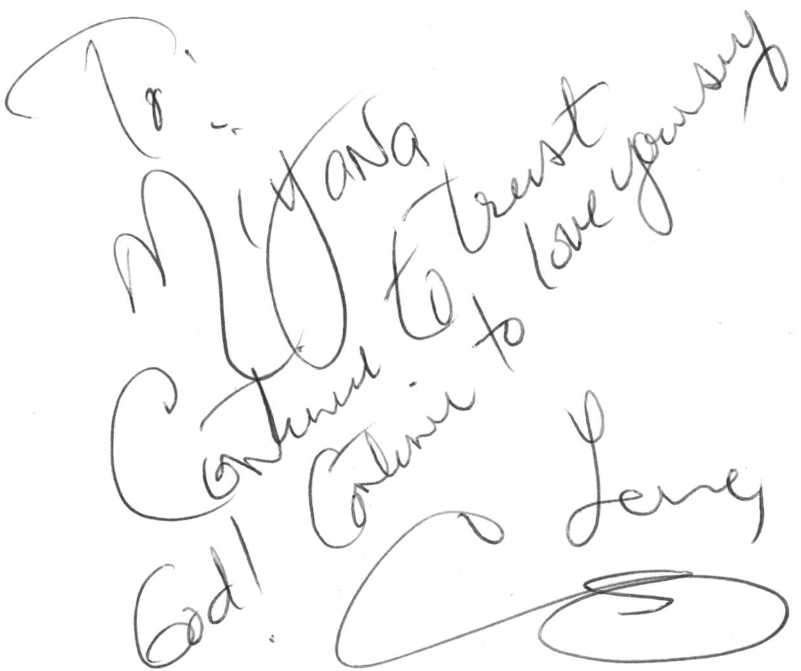

BY CANDACE YVETTE COLE

ISBN: 0-9678779-1-1
Library of Congress Catalog Card Number: 00-90399

COLE PUBLISHING COMPANY
2690 W. IMPERIAL HWY.
SUITE 124
INGLEWOOD, CA 90303
310-821-8147

Cover Design by Paula White
Inside Illustrations by
Harlan Brewer and Hubert Sam
323-290-1421

Printed in the United States by:
Morris Publishing
3212 East Highway 30
Kearney, NE 68847
1-800-650-7888

WHAT ARE READERS SAYING ABOUT THE BOOK?

Candace Cole has once again, touched the heart through her latest creation. **DAUGHTER, There Is More To You Than Meets The Eye...** is a creative compilation of the stories of women. These stories unvail the brokeness that lies underneath the smiles of our women of yesteryears and today. These stories spotlight pain, unmask hurt, and reveal brokenness. However, these stories point toward a healer named Jesus who causes the pain to cease, and restoration to begin. These stories reveal that, not only will God heal you and make you whole, but he will use you to bring others to him.

-Pastor Camille Russell
Pastor of Discovering Your Purpose Ministry
Faithful Central Bible Church, Inglewood, CA

Daughter, There Is More To You Than Meets the Eye" is a God-send for any woman who has been battered by life's storms. Candace Cole takes women in the Bible and makes their stories modern day life lessons. Let the healing begin for all who dare to venture into the wisdom this book offers."

-Antracia Merrill, L.A. Focus
Managing Editor, Inglewood, CA

Daughter ... "When you have read this powerful depiction of truth in historical times as well as today's woman, you will either do three things. You will cry, rejoice or run. 1)You will cry because you will discover you are not alone and that God understands your pain and is willing to heal you 2)You will rejoice because the testimony of this book, confirms what God has already done on the inside of you; 3)You will run because you have come face to face with your demons and baggage and you are not willing to deal with them. If this is you, please stand still and allow God's love to heal you and show you that there is "MORE" to you than meets the eye of your plight.

-Evang. DeEtta West
WB Television Network
Los Angeles, CA

"In this dynamic book, Candace Cole deals with real issues that touch the broken, battered, bruised and even bitter women of our generation. She ushers them into a place of blessedness and wholeness in Christ Jesus. With much conviction, she boldly, unashamedly and unapologetically speaks where the church is often silent, helping the reader to appropriately and practically apply the liberating truth of God's Word to the hidden, painful places in their lives. A reading of this book won't let you accept less than God's best for you."
-Rev. Tracy Leggins, MS
Los Angeles, CA

Daughter... "brings the Word of God to life by giving a 'behind the scenes' look at God's chosen women in scripture. Revealing the universality of painful issues women have faced, dated back to scripture, Daughter... will usher you into the presence of God to release the pains of the past, grasp His unchanging love for His daughters, and will validate you as a woman of God."
- Pastor Monique Everett
Pastor of Womens' Discipleship
Faithful Central Bible Church, Inglewood, CA

Daughter, There Is More To You than Meets The Eye, "is a beautiful compilation, showing the diversity of women with struggles and triumphs. Candace has taken true women of the Bible a step further, giving us illustrations of closure to challenges and opportunities women have encountered in the past and what we must face today.

Candace brings God's daughters of His Word to life; this time, to show us truth, forgiveness, esteem, courage, and the ability to deal with ourselves, right where we are today. This modern day scribe also teaches us to look beyond ourselves and externalize, not internalize; to humbly expose ourselves as the women we are, in order to edify one another and ultimately glorify God. Thank you, Candace Cole."

- Michelle Johnson
Servant-Leader, Women's Ministry
Jordan Covenant Church, Inglewood, CA

Daughter... will take you there; take you where you ask? Take you to places you may have been reluctant to go: places of your past, your issues, your pain, your dark places of denial - <u>your places of needed healing</u>. By unmasking various biblical characters' unfeigned stories, Daughter takes you on a journey through their forgotten and/or buried life history. While reading Daughter... you may find yourself reminded of a familiar history - with your name in place of the Daughter. Yes, Daughter will take you there just to show you that "THERE IS MORE TO YOU THAN MEETS THEY EYE..."

-Pastor Anthony Miguel Johnson
Jordan Covenant Church
Inglewood, CA

ACKNOWLEDGMENTS

Daughter... was conceived and completed in April of 1997. It took four months to write her. However, because God is a God of timing, she was not due to be birthed until now, year 2000. One of the greatest joys of writing this book and preparing it for today has been the new relationships I have bridged through the editing stages. People with genuine love and care for this project, Daughter. It truly takes many individuals to see a book come into existence. I would like to thank the following persons who shared significantly in this project:

Anna Alves, Editor "My lady bug", your joyful spirit has made writing a wonderful joy and fulfillment. Thank you for demanding the absolute best and nothing less. Your insight and work has been an invaluable gift to me.

Wendy R. Wise, Assistant Editor: your friendship, sisterhood, buddy and being my assistant editor has been a blessing from the throne. God blesses each individual with people that will walk with them on their way to their destiny. I am so glad he chose you to walk with me and encourage me every step of the way. Working with you has been an incredible experience. Thank you for the growing pains. Thank you for your patience and balance.

The following persons, who completed the great task of reading the preliminary manuscript of the book, assisted me in making invaluable comments on how to improve the book:

Valerie Baynes, Kasey Bedford, Dorothy Brewer, Carstella Cook, Maurine Anderson, Charlene Maryland, Ann Colemon, Rusty Colemon(adviser), Maura Gale, Joyce Johnson, Michelle Johnson, Tracy Leggins, JoAnn Sanders, Debra Seamster, Melody Stephens, Sheila Miller, Yvonne Worrill, Linda Jones, Joy Anderson, Janet Sasser, Teresa Francis, Yvette Williams, and continual prayer by the Love and Care Ministry, Connie White thank you for covering me during this time.

Evangelist Jewell Turner, come home! I love God for our precious friendship and sisterhood that he has kept throughout these years.

To my mother, Estella Liggins, your consistent demonstration of unconditional love has always blessed me. You have been the embodiment of 1st Corinthians 13 (love) that I can actually see and touch. I love you Mommy.

To my mother Dorothy Brewer, I have grown so much through our relationship, BUT still, I know the best is yet to come, don't you. I know there is more...I love you.

Pastor Gwen Rollins, I have learned that one can never have too many spiritual mothers. Thank you for being one of my special angels (mommys) sent from God.

To: Pastor Laverne Tolbert, Pastor Monique Everett, Pastor Camille Russell, Johnnie Stewart, Allysunn Francis, my sisters in ministry. Thank you for your love, prayers and sisterhood.

Rev. Joyce Johnson thank you for the many occasions when you had to literally join God in walking with me through the valleys of the shadows of death: One should be so blessed to have a friend like you.

Teron Seay: Thank you for challenging my Godliness and my walk with the Lord. You will never know the blessing you have been to me.

Rev. Tracy Leggins, thank you for your precious insight in helping me to express my deep passions and burdens through this book.

Pastor Mary Alice Haye, your encouring spirit and reaffirming smiles continues to bless me immeasurably. Thank you.

DeEtta West, girl you know you have preached Daughter... all over this country. I thank you for truly preparing the way for it's arrival.

Michelle Johnson: If one has two or three friends in one life, they are overly blessed. God saw fit to bless me again, with a woman of God such as yourself to come along side of me and walk with me through this spiritual birthing. I thank you for hanging in there with me. I appreciate all your hard work and sacrifices that you have made to be a part of Daughter...

Tommie B. Davis: you told me that Daughter... would be special for both men and women across the globe. Thank you for your words of encouragement.

To my cousin Harlan Brewer: thank you for working so dilligently with me and providing me with the best artwork I could ever imagine. You have brought a greater deminsion and expression to my book and I am so, so grateful to God for you. I am so glad I attended our 1999 Family Reunion in August.

To Paula White, thank you for capturing the essence, spirit and the royalty of Daughter..., in your cover design. It's been a joy working with you. You can design girl.

Antracia Merrill, thank you for taking the time out of your busy schedule to share your affection for Daughter....

Mark Bates, your unconditional friendship, genuine affection, unwavering support and presence has been so special to me.

Guess what? It's a girl! Because of the enormity of this project, I may have accidentlly left out names of people who helped me along the way. If so, please know that I really do appreciate all of you and your contributions be it encouragement, critiquing, or praying during the birthing of Daughter while coming out of the creative birth canal. Thank you for helping me deliver this timely child.

SPECIAL ACKNOWLEDGEMENT

To my Pastor, Bishop Kenneth C. Ulmer and my church family: I find myself at a great loss for adequate words while attempting to express my deepest gratitude for your care, compassion and support toward my ministry. Your continual support has been more than a blessing. Thank you for all the prophetic words that you have spoken into my life while I anxiously sat back and watched them come to pass. Thank you for depositing the life transforming Word of Truth, deliverance and liberation into the soil of my soul. May God continue to bless you pastor as you continue to be a blessing to so many near and far.

SPECIAL THANKS:

The following men are Pastors that have been a God-send to be my spiritual brothers and spiritual fathers:

Sydney Butler, for your unshakeable vision and conviction in the purposes of God for my life. Scars, is on the way. I promise.
Pastor Anthony Miguel Johnson "Tae, Tae", Our 9 year friendship has been filled with genuine love, appreciation, pain, growth and lots of fun. You have been a true brother/pastor.
Pastor Lance Hardaway. Thank you for standing with me, when it felt as if I was standing all by myself with God. Your prayers and support during my transitory season, really strengthened me.
Pastor Willie McBride: Your timely presence in my life lets me know that God is a God of seasons. Our friendship has meant a lot to me and continues to.
Pastor Johnny Baylor: Sometimes it only takes one word or one phrase to lift somebody up; you have had plenty of "one liners" that have done that very thing, and you probably didn't even know it.
Pastor Austin Williams, thank you for teaching me not to despise small beginnings in the midst of my beginnings.
Pastor L.A. Kessee: You have been a great mentor and friend.
Pastor Keith Woods, your brotherly love and faithful support has encouraged me greatly throughout the years.
Quaford Colemon, for your ceaseless support, joy and celabration in my many endeavors past and present.
Pastor Alvin Isaac, your prayers and friendship has been such a joy. I thank God for you.
Pastor Jordan Allen, thank you for always believing in me and giving me your extraordinary support.
Pastor Charles Brooks, your brotherly love continues to bless me. I thank God for your ministry and your integrity to call both men and women into accountability. Blessings to you and your entire household.

"MY HEROES AND MY SHEROES IN THE FAITH"

ALVIN BREWER AND DOROTHY BREWER: I thank God for blessing me with two wonderful, loving and God fearing parents.

TED LIGGINS AND ESTELLA LIGGINS: thank you for coming to Fresno in in 1967 to impact my life forever. I will always be grateful for your love and unconditional care for me.

BISHOP T.D. JAKES It was upon your spiritual ordasity to deal with the immeasurable pain in women that caused such an erruption of deliverance in my life 5 years ago. I thank God for thrusting his vision, voice and assignment to raise up the victims and declare them victorious, and virtuously valiant in Jesus Name through you! Thank you very much for your obedience.

DR. BEVERLY "BAM" CRAWFORD - Because you pastor beyond the four walls of your church, I have been the recipient of your anointed teachings, advice, instructions and support. Please know that you have helped me in so many areas of my walk with Christ. Thank you for taking out the time to sit with me and encourage me along the way of life's many journeys filled with excitement, adventure, dissappointments, hurts and victories. Your example and declaration for excellence in the Kingdom of God has taught me to give God my very best. Thank you so much for the pearls of wisdom that you have freely given that I shall keep around my neck.

DR. CLYDE ODEN, thank you for your spiritual guidance, balance and your unconditional friendship. I also thank God for you pushing me forward to "The More in Me..." in 1992 at Ward A.M.E during my orientation. God is amazing. Our friendship throughout the years has repeatedly shown me just how much God loves me.

DR. VASHTI MURPHY MCKENZIE: The sermon you preached in 1990 "Hit The Road Jack and Don't You Come Back No More No More", dealt specifically with fear of stepping out on God's word to accept the calling on your life. I will never forget that sermon, because it was those words that God used to confirm and affirm many things in my spirit. I give God praise for your life and the legacy that you courageously live before us, "Women of Great Destiny". You have been more than a mentor to me, you have been a sister, friend across the states.

PROFESSOR RIK STEVENSON (PASTOR). I am so glad that you pushed me to go beyond the comfortable areas in scripture and search the deep things of God while in your class. I had so much fun and gained so much knowledge. My brother, professor and friend thank you for sharing your knowledge and teaching with such love and zeal.

PASTOR NORMAN D. COPELAND, thank you for your strong leadership.

PASTOR ANN LIGHTNER, great woman of God, thank you for your prayers and the blessings that you spoke into my life during the revival in 1998 at Holy Trinity A.M.E.

PASTOR MELVIN WADE: for sharing the Word of God and patiently always answering a thousand questions about the Word of God when it wasn't so clear to me. I praise God for your life and the testimony that you are.

POPPA AL SEAY AND MOMMA BETTY SEAY: God has saw fit to yet bless me with another set of parents. Words are not sufficient to describe the unspeakable joy that you are to me.

DEDICATION

With sincere compassion, I dedicate this book to women across the globe of every race, religion, culture, and age. May this book uplift your hearts, give light, and inspiration to the areas long deemed dark by life's scars and tragedies. It is my prayer that **Daughter**... allows you to see the beautiful woman and daughter you are to God. Remember, in spite of your path, you are the "Phenominal Woman" as Maya Angelou poetically declares, and you are His "Queen" as Oprah Winfrey encourages us.

FOREWORD

This book represents an important milestone in understanding the dynamics of the feminine spirit. Reverend Sister Cole, from her own unique experiences and perspectives, provides the reader with a biblical and insightful approach to responding to the life struggles of women.

It is one of Reverend Sister Cole's greatest virtues as a minister to use her own life victories and experiences as a vehicle to help the reader understand the sovereignty of God. She does not lump all emotional damage together and offer a remedy, but rather walks the reader through the process of healing. Reverend Sister Cole has a special insight into the heart of hurting women and girls.

"Daughter, There is More To You Than Meets The Eye" is a down to earth book and teaching workbook that reflects the value, worth and stamina of the feminine spirit!

Pastor Mary Alice Haye
Department of Counseling Ministries
-Member of Faithful Central Bible Church, Inglewood, CA

PREFACE

Daughter, There Is More To You Than Meets The Eye, by Candace Cole is a must reading for anyone who has experienced trouble and turmoil in their life. **Daughters**... is filled with warmth, tragedy, failure, victory, and suspense. This graphic and on occasion catastrophic dramatic portrayal of the lives first century women and their encounters with Jesus is sure to bring tears to your eyes.

Daughter... is a compelling no holds barred biblical book that delivers the accounts of six different women and their struggles to survive in a world that has not been friendly to them simply because of their gender or culture. From start to finish the reader is thrust into the lives, struggles, fears, and accomplishments of the women next door, the sister you never knew, or the little girl inside who just wanted to be loved. Candace has proven herself to be one of the up and coming dramatic writers of our time. Her pin point biblical exegesis coupled with a dose of lethal, but soothing literary savoi faire makes for heart warming non stop reading. There has not been a more intriguing personification of biblical truth since the ***SCREW TAPE LETTERS*** **Written by C.S. LEWIS.**

Daughter... is only the beginning of a collection of soon to be Best Sellers. Get it soon. They won't stay on the shelves long!

- Rik Stevenson, M.A.,Th M.
Fuller Seminary
Pasadena, CA

Introduction

Daughter, There Is More To You Than Meets The Eye is written to bring to center stage the great women of the Bible who have survived, persevered, and triumphed over unfavorable odds.

Spotlighted on the succeeding pages are depictions of common, yet traumatic struggles and of molestation, abandonment, bitterness, anger, deception, depression, and unforgiveness. Revealed herein, is the Sovereignty of God intervening in the lives of these women who have been unanimously outcast, kicked to the curb, and rendered null and void by loved ones based on society's standards. However, notice how once in the Master's hands, these same women rise to heights of prominence and power through the saving grace of God. Many stories of women found in scripture are often fragmented and incomplete. Well, **"Daughter, There Is More To You Than Meets The Eye"**, captures their true accounts, then creatively joins modern day testimonies of the same experiences giving the readers a fuller narrative from start to finish. From these stories you will discover that there is nothing new under the sun, that cannot be overcome.

I have discovered that life has many ups and downs, twists and turns, and highs and lows: Perhaps you too can attest to the following:

A. The very thing that validates ones womanhood and femininity, can also stamp a seal of disapproval and inadequacy on the front of your heart;

B. The very thing which gives one security and confidence, can also bring you doubt and discouragement;

C. The very thing which you put your trust and hope in, can also transform into deceit and betrayal;

D. The very thing which consumes you with laughter and joy may fill your eyes with tears of regrets;

E. The very thing which brings you so much peace and tranquility, can suddenly turn into a vicious war of unrest;

F. The very thing which you thank God for every morning, can cause you to have some long days and some sleepless nights;

G. The very thing that causes you to blush, tremble, and make your heart palpitate, can be the same thing that causes you to crawl up in a room, depressed and ashamed to be alive.

If you can attest to any of the preceding experiences, this book is for you. Before you read another line, you must realize that,

"Daughter, There Is More To You Than Meets The Eye."

You may ask, the eye of what?

1. The eye of every **r**ejection you've experienced.
2. The eye of every **b**rutal physical attack you've endured.
3. The eye of every **h**eartbreak you've had.
4. The eye of every **p**ain you've suffered.
5. The eye of every **a**buse, emotional and physically that you've survived.
6. The eye of every **f**alse accusation against you.
7. The eye of every **d**eception you've believed.
8. The eye of every **i**ncestuous and rape experience you've harbored.
9. The eye of every **i**nfidelity and betrayal you've survived.
10. The eye of every **r**eputation you've been known by.
11. The eye of every **m**istake you've made and bad choice you've selected.
12. The eye of every **a**ddiction you've had.
13. The eye of every **r**ejection and abandonment you've faced.
14. The eye of every **f**oster home you've lived in.
15. The eye of every **s**uicide attempt you've tried.
16. The eye of every **j**ail cell you've been locked in.
17. The eye of every **c**hild you've had out of wedlock.
18. The eye of every **a**bortion you've had to go through.
19. The eye of every **mi**scarriage you've suffered.

20. The eye of every **n**o show on the wedding date.
21. The eye of every **d**ivorce court you've stood in.

And so on......

Yes, there is <u>more</u> to you than the experiences of your past or present troubles. Although the enemy has tried to make you feel like a loser, an outcast, and a mistake, please know that you were created by the hand of God, and He has a great plan for your life.

Is this book for you? **Daughter, There Is More To You Than Meets The Eye** is more than just a catchy title, its content offers truth and promises to every women who struggles with believing she cannot escape the strongholds of her past and present.

It is therefore my intention and desire that this book will be one of many resources that will cause women universally to **LIFT** their sights on high, and see themselves in a greater light and purpose, as God does.
Now, I encourage you to travel the pages of **Daughter, There Is More To You Than Meets The Eye,** as these powerful women reveal their stories and the transforming, powerful love of God.

-Candace Yvette Cole

CHAPTER 1
"A REPENTANT MOTHER AND A FORGIVING DAUGHTER"

II SAMUEL 13:1-20(KJV)

1) And it came to pass after this, that Absalom, the son of David, had a fair sister, whose name was Tamar; And Amnon the son of David loved her.

2) And Amnon was so distressed that he fell sick for his sister, Tamar; for she was a virgin. And Amnon thought it hard for him to do anything to her.

3) But Amnon had a friend, whose name was Jonadab, the son of Shimeah, David's brother; and Jonadab was a very subtle man.

4) And he said unto him, Why art thou, being the king's son, lean from day to day? Wilt thou not tell me? And Amnon said unto him, I love Tamar, my brother Absalom's sister.

5) And Jonadab said unto him, Lay thee down on thy bed and pretend that thou art sick; and when thy father cometh to see thee, say unto him, I pray thee, let my sister, Tamar, come, and give me food, and prepare the food in my sight, that I may see it, and eat it at her hand.

6) So Amnon lay down, and pretended that he was sick; and when the king was come to see him, Amnon said unto the king, I pray thee, let Tamar, my sister, come, and make me a couple of cakes in my sight that I may eat at her hand.

7) Then David sent home to Tamar saying, Go now to thy brother Amnon's house, and prepare a meal for him.

8) So Tamar went to her brother Amnon's house; and he was laid down, and she took flour and kneaded it, and made cakes in his sight, and did take the cakes.

9) And she took a pan, and poured them out before him; but he refused to eat. And Amnon said have out all men from me. And they went out every man from him.

10) And Amnon said unto Tamar, Bring the food into the chamber, that I may eat of thine hand. And Tamar took the cakes which she had made, and brought them into the chamber to Amnon, her brother.

11) And when she had brought them unto him to eat, he took hold of her, and said unto her, come, lie with me, my sister.

12) And she answered him, Nay, my brother, do not force me; for no such thing ought to be done in Israel. Do not thou this folly.

13) And I, where shall I cause my shame to go? And as for thee, thou shalt be as one of the fools in Israel. Now, therefore, I pray thee, speak unto the king; for he will not withhold me from thee.

14) However, he would not heed to her voice; and being stronger than she, he forced her and lay with her.

15) Then Amnon hated her exceedingly, so that the hatred with which he hated her was greater than the love with which he had loved her. And Amnon said unto her, "Arise, be gone!"

16) So she said to him, "No, indeed! This evil of sending me away is worse than the other that you did to me." But he would not listen to her.

17) Then he called his servant that ministered unto him, and said, put now this woman out from me, and bolt the door after her.

18) And she had a garment of several colors upon her; for with such robes were the king's daughters who were virgins, apparelled. Then his servant brought her out, and bolted the door after her.

19) And Tamar put ashes on her head and tore her garment of several colors that was on her, and laid her hand on her head, and went on her way, crying.

20) And Absalom, her brother, said unto her, hath Amnon, thy brother, been with thee? but hold now thy peace, my sister. He is thy brother; regard not this thing. So Tamar remained desolate in her brother Absalom's house.

***

Hi, my name is Michal. I am Tamar's mother. You have just read the insidious account of my daughter being raped by her stepbrother Amnon. In this incident, everyone in our household had a say regarding this tragedy, except for me. King David, Tamar's father, just got angry and shut down. Absalom, Tamar's brother sought revenge and eventually assassinated Amnon for raping his baby sister. As for me, I was the silent voice that chose not to speak at all on the matter. Allow me to give you a little background on our family. My marriage to King David was based solely on a political arrangement that my father orchestrated. In that day marriages between powerful political families served as a way to seal treaties, alliances, and other covenants. Regardless of my father's ulterior motive in giving me in marriage to King David, I genuinely loved David with all of my heart. I respected him at all costs, and I tried to stand by him to protect his name and his reputation, even at the cost of not protecting my own flesh and blood, my daughter, Tamar. I remained silent, non-responsive, tucked away in the royal palace, as my daughter was rushed into hiding at her brother Absalom's house.

Well, everyone has at least one or two regrets in their life, that if given the opportunity to do it all over again, would. And so, today, I wish to repent for my own silent actions and stand in proxy on behalf of parents who also did not have the courage or ability to come to the aid of their little sons and daughters when they needed them the most. I don't know their reasons, but mine were clear. I was caught up in my royal status, and man. King David was a great man of honor, status, reputation and pride. Regrettably, I made a choice, like so many other mothers and fathers to sweep the truth underneath a carpet of shame and denial, to keep the peace and avoid scandal. As a result, I did not speak to my daughter for approximately twenty years.

Throughout the years, I would inquire about her from time to time from nearby neighbors, and I learned that Tamar lived a life filled with depression and continual sickness.

I also learned mistakes have a way of staying with you, no matter how hard you try to forget them. You can't tuck them away, you can't excuse them away, you can't lie them away, you can't deny them away, you can't drink them away, and you certainly can't make them go away. Mistakes just seem to always resurface from your attempts to make them vanish.

One day while sitting on my royal throne, God revealed to me the additional damage I contributed to my daughter's life by my silence and withdrawal from her. Oh, how I wished I had the chance to do it all over again! God continued to admonish me to go to my daughter and confess my willful negligence of my responsibility to protect her as a mother should.

I knew I needed to go talk with my daughter and finally apologize to her for my absence and silence all these years. I struggled with my fear and pride and begged God to remove anything in me that would prevent me from doing His will.

I pressed past the bondage of shame with God's help and sought to go see about my daughter. It wasn't easy, but I was determined.

A nurse answered the door when I arrived at Tamar's house and told me she was bedridden. After receiving Tamar's permission to enter her bedroom, I slowly walked in. The nurse readjusted her bed to a sitting position, and I laid eyes on my beloved daughter for the first time in almost 20 years.

I stood in the doorway not able to come any closer due to my uncertainty and inward shame that only an absent mother would feel. I looked at her face which had not changed other than with age. The last time I laid eyes on my baby, she was 13 years old. Her hair was still long and beautiful as it was twenty years ago. Her voice however, was weak as a faint whisper. I didn't delay my visit by making pointless and nervous small talk. I just proceeded to say these words:

> "Tamar, Momma is so sorry your brother raped you. I regret I was not there to hold you and wipe the tears from your eyes. I am sorry I was not there to help you remove the clothes that were torn off your little frail body, or to wash the ashes off of your face from your shame and pain. Baby, I could have reaffirmed your dignity and self worth. I know I made a foolish decision to not come to your side, but I couldn't see beyond my own pious status and royal throne. Instead, I quietly sat back as the days of your youth painfully roll by. Only God knows the depth of your pain and agony. I missed your birthdays and so many other important days. I know your plans were shattered within moments of that one selfish violation.

God if I could just turn back the hands of time.

"Tamar, I realize now that your life would have been so different if I would have just been there for you. I know that my love should have saved you from thinking you were worthless and dead inside. In spite of what happened to you, I should have told you that I still loved you. It was my responsibility as a parent to make sure you had a home and a safe environment. When you struggled with wondering if anyone cared, I should have been the one to stand up when no one else would."

Though the words I spoke were so hard for me to say, it seemed as if God was pouring the words directly out from my soul. I continued.

"Tamar, you need to know that you are still a princess in my heart and in God's eyes. That evil act did not take that away, because your Heavenly Father, your Creator, is the God of Gods and the Lord of Lords and the King of Kings. It is His divine royal blood that runs through your veins. Tamar, I hate I didn't tell you that I believed your report when your brother tried to tell everybody a different story. I know it was not your fault baby."

While listening, Tamar turned her head slightly away from me looking toward her window. I could see the tears slowly rolling down the side of her face, and it hurt me to see her hurt. I wanted so desperately to hold her in my arms, but I remained at the doorway.

"Baby, can you hear me?"

Still looking away, she slowly nodded her head indicating she could.

"Tamar, you're beautiful and precious. You are a rose amidst a garden of thorns. It's not your fault Satan had a scheme against your life to destroy you."

By now, I too was crying.

“I regret that I didn’t let you know sooner, that God could heal your pain, but the greatest regret I have is not being a true mother to you all these years.”

As the muffled moans of pain rose from her, tears rolled down her face like a running faucet longing to be released.

“Tamar, can you ever forgive your mother?”

The room was quiet and still. She slowly turned toward me, her trembling voice whispered, “Yes Momma, I forgive you.” Then she reached out to me as a little child needing a Mommy’s embrace. I ran to her bedside holding her tight against my breast stroking her silky black hair. I held her for hours, and we wept together. I then continued to speak “life” into her, while she stayed buried in the locks of my shoulders.

“Tamar, did you know that God named you when you were in my womb? Your name means "Palm", like the Palm trees. You know that Palm trees are survivors of the worst storms of life. They survive through hurricanes, vicious winds, and rainstorms. The palm tree is one of the strongest trees of God's creation. Unlike the oak tree whose durability cannot withstand persistent winds that causes it to uproot itself. Also, unlike the mulberry tree which is deciduous, and sheds leaves in autumn and is not lasting because it falls down and falls back! Baby, the palm tree, though it is the most fragile and gets the most abuse, it always stands the test of the storms it faces.

And though you have been hit with a whirlwind of confusion and pain Tamar, you survived. Though your world has been devastated with fear and trembling from the attack of the enemy, you survived. Emotional hurricanes tried to uproot your identity and self esteem, but you survived. Though the storms flooded you with shame and humiliation, trying to wash away your purity, but guess what? You survived. You survived even when family shunned you and cast you away. Yes, life has violently tried to blow you down, but you didn't fall back or break. Instead you survived. Why Tamar? Because you are like the tree planted by the rivers of water. You shall not be moved; you will stand. Your leaves shall not wither, but bring forth fruit in its season. I know you have suffered a long time, but your due season has just rolled around and God declares unto you that you shall not die, but live and declare the wonderful works of the Lord."

That day marked the beginning of our new beginning as mother and daughter. I still rejoice when I think about that timely and unforgettable visit with Tamar. Since then, we have bonded so much. Seemingly, we picked up right where we left off. Her childlike humorous side had returned and I could once again enjoy the youthful laughter that I once heard as she and her friends played in the garden. However, I will not say that our reunion days were all peaches and cream, but I will say that we worked through the issues of health, forgiveness, and restoration.

Tamar had to work through anger and the stages of unforgiveness. I watched her as she displayed being torn between love and hate. Sometimes she would hate to be around me because it reminded her of when I wasn't around. Then there were times that she would smother me with hugs and kisses; she had unpredictable mood swings to say the least. Throughout our venting sessions discussing the past, Tamar expressed deep anger and frustrations toward my past selfish acts and careless decisions. Those were the most painful words I had ever heard, but they were absolutely the naked truth. I wanted to tell her to leave it all in the past and walk forward, but I realized that to would have been selfish and insensitive on my behalf. Because of her pain, she warranted the opportunity to be able to say whatever was on her mind. I had to understand that she had to live with her pain for over two decades, and I just couldn't tell her to get over it, because it was making me feel uncomfortable! Thank God for the wisdom to hold my tongue before I dig myself into a deeper hole.

Tamar's health gradually improved as time went on. She didn't have as many emergencies as in the past. I accompanied her on one of her doctor's visits and spoke with the doctor privately to understand my daughters total condition. I was shocked to learn what he believed to be the primary contributing factor to her condition. He spoke about her life long depression and the affects of unresolved emotional pain which translates into unforgiveness. He gave me profound facts about medical repercussions emanating from unforgiveness in the heart.

Being familiar with our family, her doctor recommended that I call a family reunion together and pursue creative ways to bring about some healthy resolutions from the issues of our past. He concluded by saying, "People just don't understand the power of talking out issues and humbling oneself before one another."

I took the advice of the doctor and planned for the family to fellowship at the palace. Everyone was present. For some, discussing the dark shadows of our painful royal legacy was quite unbearable, but everyone stayed. Initially, trying to break the awkwardness, I began by sharing my first day with Tamar and what God gave me the strength to say and do. I talked about the fact that I had to be willing to lay aside my pride and guilt and admit to my daughter that I blew it. I then made a general apology to all of my children for any pain, trauma, and misfortune I caused them.

I believe with my heart and soul, God gives parents the power to right any wrong with the power of love and humility which leads us to provide the environment for healing through our repentance. So I beg and plead with you, if God has blessed you with children, love yourself and them enough to bring love and healing to your family so that they can be free of all the secret pains and oppressions.

TAMAR SPEAKS:

My sisters and brothers, you who have been molested or raped, please allow me to speak into your life just for a few moments. Though your pain is real and your anger is justified, you must believe that there is life after rape and molestation. I want to briefly share what my life was like before the bondage of unforgivness was released. I was a young 13 year old virgin princess waiting for the promised hour of my inheritance and future treasures that were due to me as an heiress to the royal family of David.

I proudly wore my royal garments of colors symbolizing my identity and status until that dreadful day. As you read, my stepbrother Amnon, pretended he was sick just to get me over to his small palace. Once I was there, I discovered it was all a lie. I can still hear and feel him tearing my clothes off like an animal out of control. What he didn't realize was that he not only tore off my physical garments, but he also tore my inward garments bearing my identity, my purity, my dignity, my femininity and innocence. After he raped me, he ripped me into emotional jagged pieces when he demanded his guardsmen to, "Get this thing out of here." He was referring to me. Then he could no longer stand to see me in his presence. I still remember how he shoved me out of the bed with his feet as he turned his back on me. On that day, I felt like my life was taken from me, leaving only a form with no substance or life. My voice was cut off, and I could no longer speak.

I was acquainted for the first time in my life with that horrible word called "shame." From that day forward, I spent most of my entire life hiding behind closed doors ashamed to be seen. When your life is driven by shame, hiding becomes your constant endeavor. I found myself hiding behind my dark clothes so as to not draw any attention to myself. Besides, I didn't fit the qualifications of wearing my royal garments which symbolized purity and virginity anymore. I also began eating to the point of almost bursting wide open. No matter how full I was, I was still empty, lonely and afraid inside. Once I'd leave a public environment, my world shut down into silent desolation and depression.

As I awakened each morning, the depression was right there waiting for me. My mind was tormented day and night with the whole scene of my stepbrother raping me and throwing me out in the street locking the door behind me.

From that moment on, it seemed as if everyone locked me out. There was not one person except for my brother Absalom to care for me. His solution was just as bad as my mother's silence. He asked me to keep it quiet and just politely go away and stay at his house to protect our royal household name. I didn't know it then, but I do know now that he was saying "Don't hurt." "Don't make a fuss," "Don't regard it as important, don't make other people feel uncomfortable because of it, and "Don't let it be known." "Keep it secret."

I learned over the years that his solution was unfair and insensitive. It caused me to handle my pain in an entirely unrealistic and emotionally unhealthy manner. Silence was not the cure! I needed to be able to talk, to cry and maybe even scream to at least one person who had enough real time to care. Lastly, I needed to hear my family and friends say that it was wrong, and that they cared for my well being. I did not need to be concerned with who it made uncomfortable, and whose name was on the line. Especially, when my very life and identity were already on the line hanging by sheer threads. Instead I had to be tucked away privately out of sight and out of mind, while my emotions stayed in securely bottled up inside of me. Those emotions festered day after day, month after month for years until I had a major heart condition that I didn't realize was directly related to my trauma. I discovered this after being rushed for an emergency visit to our family doctor.

That particular morning I woke up not being able to breathe and experiencing gripping pains in my chest. My doctor asked about my family history as it related to heart conditions. I answered all of his historical background questions. Then, he asked if I were happy. I just nodded, yes. Then he asked if there were any emotional or traumatic issues in my life. I started crying and getting angry at him for asking me personal questions that didn't make sense to me. I didn't understand how my chest pains were even remotely connected to family affairs. He pressed the point of asking me if I had any anger or unforgiveness in my heart that I was aware of. I nearly fainted.

Well to make a long story short, I refused to admit to any problems in my royal family. After all, who did not know King David and all of his royal children? He prescribed a mild nerve relaxer to keep me calm and asked me to come see him in two weeks.

Before I left, he said he felt compelled to inform me of important statistics directly relating to anger and unforgiveness. He said that it had been medically proven that unforgiveness was the number one killer in the history of all humankind. Further, he said it was a silent epidemic found in families across the world. Its symptoms are hard to detect, but it manifests itself in many forms such as heart disease, high blood pressure, depression, arthritis, back problems, lupus, multiple sclerosis, strokes, and various forms of cancer. It eats at the core of your body from the inside out, from the top of your head to the soles of your feet. It roams your body to find a doorway to cripple you and kill you.

I have to admit, he put something on my mind that day. That which was deeply embedded in my spirit was now seeping out of the seams of my life, affecting my health.

May I say to you that I believe this is the enemy's ultimate way of destroying your life as if the initial tragedy was not enough. If he can get you to hate your abuser and keep your mind consumed with the memory of the act, then he's got control over your spirit and emotions. If he can keep bitterness, unforgiveness, and anger simmering inside of you, he has accomplished his entire mission. The first mission being the violation, the second mission your being tormented with bitterness and unforgiveness. I was on my way to the final kill. The next step was death.

Well, that was my life in a nutshell until my mother walked in my bedroom one afternoon and stopped the cankerworm from eating my soul alive. She came that day just to ask me to forgive her for abandoning me all those years. Then she asked me to forgive her and let her be the mother she desired to be, though she was too afraid and ashamed to come sooner. Now, I had two decisions to make. Would I hold on to the anger and unforgiveness that I had harbored deeply in my heart, or would I forgive her and enjoy the rest of my life with the mother that I had been missing for all those years? This would mean immediate relief for her, but what would it mean for me? I struggled in those moments because I didn't know if I could trust her. Could I open my heart up to her again? Would she abandon me again? Fear totally came over me. Then in a split second, I heard a still small voice whisper "Forgive her. You can trust me, and you can be free". I can still remember the tears flowing like a running river and me reaching toward my Mommy, reaching for the arms that had not held me for years. The words my mother spoke as she gently held me in her arms, compelled emotional chains to drop from my mind and released my heart to receive her repentance. At that moment, the choice I made to forgive, changed me and freed my soul. I felt that I had been surgically and miraculously healed by God to open my heart to love again and trust again.

This freed my mother also and took the chains of guilt and shame away from her. She suggested that my freedom and liberation would triumph in its fullness as I walked the same steps of confronting my fears, doubts and my angers as she did. At that moment, she gave me a license to be real with myself, with her, and more importantly with God. She offered me a safe environment to verbally release all that had been locked up on the inside of me. She told me that forgiveness is essential, but it is a process that we must walk out of, and not run through.

My mother and I began a new spiritual journey with her as my mentor. Our new relationship started there and we have been inseparable ever since. Notice I said earlier that God did a miracle in me. I don't want you to miss what the miracle was. It was the opening of my heart to trust, to love again and to receive love.

My mother and I spent the remaining days of our relationship working out the pains of our past through a joint commitment to counseling, open communication, prayer, and continuing diligently to love each other in the midst of it all. The process was worth the journey to finally get the love we both deserved and needed.

I also struggled in my relationship with God because I felt he had abandoned me too. I guess I was angry with Him. For the first time in my life, I understood that just because God is all powerful, doesn't mean He is the blame for all tragedies that humans experience. More importantly, He is the healer of all our wounds if we can believe and let Him.

I give praise and glory to God for His power to restore me and my family. Does forgiveness heal a person? Yes, and it empowers you to walk in new strength by the power of God.

While, I know forgiveness doesn't always require one to physically reconcile with a particular person due to circumstances, it is still possible. For example, if the person is deceased, you can still reconcile with God and release those old feelings to Him as I had to do for my stepbrother Amnon who died before I forgave him.

Finally, once you allow the initial seed of love and forgiveness to be activated in you, then you know you are becoming free. You will discover nothing can hold you back once you're free. Once tragedies in your life cannot limit your future, then you know you're free. Once you discover that there is vision beyond the anger and the bitterness, then you know you are free. Once you discover and realize that your life and destiny is in the hands of God, then no demon in hell can prevail against it. There is no abuse, no violation or attack that can define you and disqualify you and make God disown you. Once you know that God is the one who defines your worth, importance, and purpose, then you too can shout the Victory!

You will remember that I asked my Amnon one last question before he raped me: "Where shall my shame go?" Well, I finally got my answer after all these years: God says, "it goes to Him."

* * *

CHAPTER 1
A REPENTANT MOTHER AND A FORGIVING DAUGHTER
SELAH! PAUSE, LIFE LESSONS

Tamar finally discovered where she could put her shame, and it wasn't behind closed doors, underneath dark oversized clothes, nor was it in compulsive eating. She put her shame in the loving arms of God who declares, "When mother and father hath forsaken you, then I will take you up."(Psalms 27:10) Yes, Jehovah Rophe, God our healer is able to heal the hurts that we don't deserve* and to bring joy into our lives through the uncompromising power of forgiveness. And we too, like Tamar have been given a place to put the shame of our lives which the enemy wants to lord over our heads trying to make us feel dirty, unclean, and unworthy. God's love covers a multitude of sin and shame. How and Where? Over 2,000 years ago, God sent his only begotten son, Jesus Christ who died on a hill called Calvary. He was nailed to the cross for the sin of the world, but not only our sin, but our shames, pains, sicknesses, losses and so much more, that by believing in Him, we shall have new life and life more abundantly.

Old things will pass away and behold all things become new. (II Corin. 5:17) Through the power of the shed blood of Jesus Christ, we are given new life, new sight, a new walk, a new destiny, and we become a new person.

Therefore, we too do not have to hide from the shame that shames us. We can come out from behind alcohol, drugs, unhealthy relationships, depression, isolation, bitterness, hatred and unforgiveness and walk in the boldness of our Lord and Savior Jesus Christ who died on a cross for our sin and shame. God is calling for us to come out of hiding and to stand in his light which overshadows any darkness that may be in our lives. God's love can cover that entire ugly thing that happened to you.

How do we do it? We must be willing to release the pains of our past and embrace the promises of our path to a loving Savior as demonstrated in our story. We witness a mother who comes to terms with the mistakes of her choices, and moves to reconcile the long damaged relationship with her daughter, expressing her love and asking her for forgiveness. This act opened the heart of her daughter to forgive. We also see a daughter humbling herself and being willing to forgive, thereby, allowing the relationship to be restored and healed.

We can still be free, even if people are not willing to own their part of the pain by releasing their heart to God and asking God to forgive through us. What is forgivness? Forgiveness is courage. Forgiveness is the perfect will of God. Forgiveness is walking away, not having to get even and tie the score of the hurt done to you. In the best seller, Forgive and Forget, Lewis B. Smedes says,

> "When we forgive we ride the crest of love's cosmic wave; we walk in stride with God. And we heal the hurt we never deserved."

If we lay aside our pride, self-pity, and fears and do as the wise, repentant, and humbled mother and daughter did, what would this world look like? What would our homes look like? What would our children look like? If we would just learn how to forgive one another, what would our communities look like?

God is concerned with our pain and our shame for He declares by telling us in

> Isaiah 54:4 Fear not; for thou shalt not be ashamed: neither be though confounded: for thou shall not be put to shame: for though shalt forget the shame of thy youth and shall not remember the reproach of thy widowhood anymore.

Then God promises us in

> Isaiah 61:7, that "for your shame ye shall have double; and for your confusion they shall rejoice in their portion: therefore in their land they shall possess the double; everlasting joy shall be unto them.

Then we can individually and corporately rejoice because in Joel 2:25-26, God declares “And I will restore to you the years that the locust hath eaten and the cankerworm, and the caterpillar, and the palmerworm, my great army which I sent among you. And ye shall eat in plenty, and be satisfied, and praise the name of the Lord your God, that hath dealt wondrously with you; and my people shall never be ashamed!

> Matthew 6:14 says “if we forgive men their trespasses, your heavenly father will also forgive you.”

Perhaps you, or someone you know have broken relationships. If so, I encourage you to become an instrument of reconciliation to your family and turn the course of your family’s destiny into an entirely different direction. At least plant the seed that will follow into the next generation.

When we decide to forgive, forgiveness creates a passport to ultimate freedom and the healing that we need from the inside out. That’s when our future begins.

CHAPTER 1
A REPENTANT MOTHER
Q & A'S

(You may choose more than one answer)

1. What did Amnon do to Tamar?
   a) Raped her
   b) Shamed her
   c) Rejected her
   d) All of the above
   Other:____________________________

2. Why did Absalom tell Tamar to go to his house?
   a) To protect the family reputation
   b) Because he wanted to rape her
   c) Fear for her life
   d) Hide her and protect her
   Other:____________________________

3. What last question did Tamar ask her brother before he raped her?
   a) Where shall my shame go?
   b) Why are you doing this to me?
   c) Why don't you go and ask permission for me?
   d) Do you love me?
   Other:____________________________

4. What is shame?
   a) Outcast
   b) Embarrassment
   c) Humiliation
   d) Disgrace
   Other:____________________________

5. What did Tamar do after her brother locked her out of his house?
a) Cried
b) Put ashes on her head
c) Tore her royal garments
d) All of the above
Other:______________________________

6. Why do you think Amnon's love turned into hatred?
a) Because it was really lust
b) He was faced with his own sin
c) He regretted what he had done
d) He felt ashamed
Other:______________________________

7. What's the difference between lust and love?

8. How do you feel the silence from Tamar's family defined how she felt about herself?
a) Desolate
b) Dirty, unaccepted, outcast
c) Disconnected from the family
d) Unloved
e) All of the above
Other:______________________________

9. How did this story make you feel?
a) Sympathetic for mothers and daughters
b) Angry at mother
c) Angry at Amnon
d) Angry at Father
e) Other:______________________________

10. Have you ever been molested or raped?

11. If your answer is yes, how have you healed from this trauma? Or how have you dealt with this trauma?
a) Counseling
b) Prayer
c) Not thinking about it
d) Still hating the person who did it
e) Other:____________________

12. How did her brother Absalom contribute to her pain, when he said "disregard this thing after all he is your brother?"
a) Made her feel unworthy of help
b) Caused her great pain
c) Made her happy
d) It broke her heart
e) Other:______________________

13. Tamar's mother came to her after 20 years to do what?
a) Repent to her and ask for forgiveness
b) Explain her absence
c) Tell her off
d) To hold her
e) All of the above
f) Other:________________________________

14. What should mothers do for their children when they are subject to their mistakes, bad choices and decisions?
a) Talk to them about it
b) Keep hiding it
c) Repent and restore relationships
d) Deny anything is wrong
e) Other:________________________________

15. What did the presence of Tamar's mother do for her?
a) Healed her
b) Gave her hope
c) Released her from burdens
d) Restored hope in her

16. Where did Tamar's shame go?

17. Are there any areas of your life that you are ashamed of?

18. How is your relationship with your mother or caretaker?

19. Do you have any unresolved issues that need to be forgiven?

20. What can the act of forgiveness do for a person ?

21. What is forgiveness?

22. When we hold things in and choose not to forgive, what are the repercussions?
    a) Sickness and disease
    b) You will not be forgiven by God
    c) You win the grudge race
    d) All of the above
    e) Other:______________________________

23. According to Isaiah 61: 1-3 what heals the bondage of pain and shame?
    a) Love
    b) Restoration
    c) Vindication
    d) God's love
    e) The loving Savior Jesus Christ
    f) Other:______________________________

What does the Bible instruct us to do if we have a quarrel against someone according to Mark 11:25?

____

If we obey Mark 11:25, what will God do for us?

____

According to Ephesians 4:32 who provides us the example of forgiveness?

Do you believe that forgiveness is a process?
Yes or No

Is there anyone in your life that you need to forgive?
Yes or No

Because it is God who gives us the power and the love to forgive others, list the name(s) of persons that you need God to help you forgive.

____________________ ________________________
____________________ ________________________
____________________ ________________________
____________________ ________________________
____________________ ________________________

In your own words, explain the process of forgiveness.

____
____
____

1st John 1:9 gives us a clear picture of the act of God forgiving us. Meditate on this scripture.

The Bible explains the initial steps to forgiveness in Mark 11:25. Study this verse, and meditate on it. Then pray that God would grant you the strength and love to forgive.

Are you ready to begin the process?
Yes or No

HLEHEM

CHAPTER 2
NAOMI, WHO ARE YOU MAD AT?

Ruth 1:1-21(KJV)

1) Now it came to pass in the days when the judges ruled that there was a famine in the land. And a certain man of Bethlem-Judah went to sorjourn in the country of Moab. He, and his wife and two sons.

2) And the name of the man was Elimelech and the name of his wife was Naomi, and the name of his sons Mahlon and Chilion, Ephratities of Bethlem-Judah. And they came with the country of Moab, and continued there.

3) Then Elimelech, Naomi's husband, died; and she was left, and her two sons

4) Now they took wives of the women of Moab; the name of the one was Orpah, and the name of the other Ruth. And they dwelt there about ten years.

5) Then both Mahlon and Chilion also died; so the woman survived her two sons and her husband.

6) Then she arose with her daughters in law that she might return from the country of Moab, for she had heard in the country of Moab that the Lord had visited His people by giving them bread.

7) Therefore she went out from the place where she was, and her two daughters in law with her, and they went on the way to return to the land of Judah.

8) And Naomi said to her two daughters in law, "Go return each to her mother's house, the Lord deal kindly with you as you have dealt with the dead and with me.

9) The Lord grant that you may find rest, each in the house of her husband. So she kissed them, and they lifted up their voices and wept.

10) And they said to her, surely we will return with you to your people."

11) But Naomi said, "Turn back, my daughters; why will you go with me? Are there still sons in my womb, that they may be your husbands?

12) Turn back, my daughters, go for I am too old to have a husband. If I should say I have hope, if I should have a husband tonight and should also bear sons,

13) Would you wait for them til they were grown? Would you restrain yourselves from having husbands? No, my daughters, for it grieves me very much for your sakes that the hand of the Lord has gone out against me!"

14) Then they lifted up their voices and wept again; and Orpah kissed her mother in law, but Ruth clung to her.

15) And she said, "Look, your sister-in-law has gone back to her people and to her gods; return after your sister in law

16) But Ruth said "entreat me not to leave you, or to turn back from following after you; for wherever you go, I will go; and where you lodge, I will lodge; your people shall be my people. And your God, my God.

17) Where you die, I will die, and there will I be buried. The Lord do so to me, and more also, if anything but death parts you and me.

18) When she saw that she was determined to go with her, she stopped speaking to her.

19) Now the two of them went until they came to Bethlehem. And it happened, when they had come to Bethlehem, that all the city was excited because of thee, and the women said, Is this Naomi?

20) But she said to them, Do not call me Naomi; call me Mara, for the Almighty has dealt very bitterly with me.

21) I went out full, and the Lord has brought me home again empty. Why do you call me Naomi, since the Lord has testified against me, and the Almighty has afflicted me.

***

Hello, I am the angry woman in the story that you just read. My name was Naomi which means "pleasant", but as you have read, I changed it to Mara which means "bitter". Please read on and you will understand why I changed my name.

How did it all start? Well, it was the season that Bethlehem experienced a famine in the land. We would have no food nor any nutritional resources to survive. My husband decided to do what any good husband would do for his family. He packed us up and said we were headed toward Moab where there was sufficient food, shelter, and work. We knew it would only be temporary until the famine lifted in Bethlehem. Then we would return home at harvest time. Friends and family did not want us to go, particularly to Moab because it was a heathen nation filled with heathen gods. The men of Bethlehem told my husband that he was going to get us killed because of the bad experience that happened during the wilderness days with our forefathers coming out of Egypt. My husband did not tarry, but kept going with his plans as scheduled.

My husband, Elimelech was a hard working man. I understood his pride as a husband and provider for his household. He believed in being the man and making sure his family was taken good care of. That was one of the things I loved about him. He was the very image and epitome of God's man and spiritual covering over his house.

Not long after our arrival in Moab, tragedy stormed at our doors afflicting my beloved husband with an internal disease. We didn't know what it was. All we could do was pray to God. I prayed night and day as I watched his condition worsen. I prayed and fasted, crying out to God even the more. It was so painful to see him suffer like that. He was such a good man, he didn't deserve to go through this trauma. Then one morning, after weeks of suffering, he died in his sleep. He was gone. I just knew God would heal him! I knew it, I believed it, and I expected it! But he died. The only man I ever loved was gone. What would I do? I couldn't believe this was happening to me. Not now! I cried out to God after holding my husband's dead body in my arms. I don't know when, but I wasn't ready for him to go then. My sons stayed by my side and took care of me. I had many painful days and nights missing my husband and trying to accept his death. I slowly began to accept my husband's death after the first year that he was gone. Though my sons were faithful to me the entire year, not letting me want for anything, I observed their weary, sad, countenance as they would come in from the fields making sure I was cared for.

One evening while at supper, I encouraged them to find themselves wives befitting of them. I knew that they couldn't stay with me forever. They eventually met two beautiful women from Moab. I knew it was against our customs to marry outside of our own people, but they met two of the kindest women. After our first dinner together, I gave my blessings to their marriage.

My daughters in-law promised me that they would have grandchildren that would keep me company and restore my youth. I looked forward to those days, but I was still bitter and angry for the loss of my husband. I felt nobody could ever fill that void in my life.

Then a couple of years later, tragedy knocked again. Not one, but both of my sons took ill at the same time. I went through a praying season from sun up to sun down just as I did for my husband. Their wives learned how to pray and intercede by watching me cry out to my God. However, my sons conditions worsened as their father's had and then they too, died. Even though I prayed as hard as I could for my sons, God took them anyway. I felt God was not hearing me and was not caring for my heart. I thought to myself, I will never pray another prayer in my life for anyone or anything. God disappointed me. I thought I was special to Him and that I could ask Him anything and it would be granted. What was I supposed to do now? An old woman in age, feeble in body with no means of providing for herself or her two widowed daughters-in-law. There were no more men or sons in our lives. On top of that, my sons were not married long enough to start a family with their wives.

From time to time, I couldn't help but wonder if we were being punished for leaving Bethlehem and going to a foreign land where there were foreign gods. I blamed myself for not talking Elimelech out of leaving. Maybe, he and my sons would be alive today if this was God's judgement. I wondered to myself. My daughters-in-laws told me that I shouldn't blame myself. I didn't know who else to blame. It was either me or God. I was so lonely. I had nothing to live for and nothing to give to my daughters-in-law. I felt so useless and empty inside. I knew I had to go back home now. I tried to send my daughters-in-law back to their parents' homes before I left. Orpah returned home to her people, but Ruth insisted that she would return to Bethlehem with me. I could not persuade her otherwise, so I let her come with me.

The journey was going to be long. We had to sell and leave all of our belongings because we had nothing on which to transport them. I tried not to think about it, because I could feel my emotions stirring up inside of me.

The trail we took reminded me of the first time I traveled with my husband, Elimelech, and my two sons, Mahlon, and Chilion when we were first coming to Moab. It's amazing how landmarks, roads, and places trigger old memories in your mind. I felt so abandoned and alone as I climbed the steep hills and rocky roads. There were times when I just wanted to turn around and go back to Moab, but realizing we had come too far to turn back, we pressed our way through the rural wilderness from one city to the next.

Trying to take our minds off the rugged trail, I talked about the joys of Bethlehem the entire way back so that Ruth could have some feel for the city and the people. She seemed to be excited. At times, I couldn't help but feel sympathy for Ruth. She was so young and had her entire life ahead of her. I watched how happy she was when she first married my son, and how her happiness suddenly turned into grief like mine. Even so, she was committed in her care and love for me. I couldn't ask for a better daughter-in-law even amongst my own people. I wanted so badly to be able to give her another son to marry. If I could do that, I would be at peace. Ruth had a lot to consider in coming to live with my people. In all honesty, it was a risk for her because our Hebrew customs were difficult enough for us, let alone an outsider. Fortunately, as a foreigner, she was entitled to numerous privileges such as the right to glean the harvest fields as long as she followed the Levitical Law. This law applied to all poor people that came into our land. However, Ruth was not simply a foreigner, but a woman, and a Moabite which made it double jeopardy. Especially because our historical law records that "no Moabite could enter the assembly of the Lord forever". This was all a result of how the Moabites sorely treated our forefathers and refused to extend bread to them as they traveled out of Egypt in the Wilderness. So you see, Ruth had no obvious reasons to believe that she would fare well in Israel, yet, she insisted on coming anyway.

On the last night of our journey before reaching Bethlehem, we ate supper in front of our makeshift fireplace. Ruth wanted to know how I was really doing regarding the experiences in Moab and now having to come home. I had to lay down my pseudo-religious front at that point. No more pronouncements to her "Oh I'm blessed", Oh praise the Lord". The truth of the matter was, I was a steam engine on the inside roaring like a mad lion. With tears flowing from my feeble eyes, I confessed," I am pretty mad at my

God right now, Ruth. Taken aback by my response, I told her I was mad at the same God that she wanted to be her God. "I am mad as hell at that God!" I repeated. I then confessed that I had been experiencing a love hate relationship with God from the time he took my husband and then my two sons. Directing my questions to her, I asked her "How could He leave me like this?" "How could He take away the only man that had ever loved me all those years and my sons and leave me with no heir?" "How could He let my heart be broken three times?" How could He let them suffer like that and then not heal their sicknesses? How could He let them slip away from me in the middle of the night, every single one? How could He fail me like this, Ruth? Pausing and catching my breath, I told her that I felt like nothing, and I didn't have anything to show for myself or my people when I returned to my homeland. I had nothing but the clothes on my back. I began to cry. How could He put me in a position of being left not once, but three times? She responded, "Mother, they didn't leave you, they died." I quickly snapped back at her, "I don't care, if it was by death or whatever, they left. They are gone, and I am still here! With what? Nothing. I am going back to a people whose questions I don't want to answer concerning my loss in Moab." Not knowing what else to do or say, she held me and told me that it would get much better once we arrived home. Ruth had never seen me so emotional. She could not believe her ears. I told her that I wouldn't always be mad at God, because I loved Him so much. I just didn't understand the "why's" that He left me with. I also told her that I am simply being real with God because, He already knew what was in my heart. I could walk around superficially saying all the sanctified phrases because that's what people are most comfortable with hearing, but I chose to be real with my feelings. We prepared to get rest for the long day's journey going into Bethlehem.

The next morning came and we continued our journey. Before night broke, I could see the city gate afar off. I nudged at Ruth as she wiped the sweat from her brow to tell her we only had a mile or so to go. Her smile lit up her steps. I glanced behind me seeing the Jericho land fading as we moved toward Bethlehem. I could see the watchmen standing on the city gates watching for intruders. The sun was starting to set on the back drop of Bethlehem as we approached the city. I could hear faint noises from the townsmen. A smile appeared on my face from the familiar to finally see people that I had not seen in over 12 years.

As we walked in the gate, women from my left and right saw me and came running to me. Those that recognized me screamed, "Is this Naomi?" Then others' screamed "Naomi's home". At first, my heart was warm but soon turned to anger after hearing the different greetings. I had so many mixed emotions stirring within me. Those that asked "Is this Naomi", were referring to my outward lowliness in countenance and body. I only had the clothes on my back. They were not used to seeing this Naomi with only meager ends with her. I just wanted to cry, but instead, I yelled out, "Do not call me Naomi!!!! All the women hushed looking surprised. You could hear a pin drop in the sands of Bethlehem. I cried out from my soul again,

> "Do not call me Naomi. Call me Mara, for the Almighty has dealt very bitterly with me. I went out full, and the Lord has brought me home again empty. Why do you call me Naomi, since the Lord has testified against me, and the Almighty has afflicted me."

I explained to them that my afflictions did not line up with the meaning of my name, and so I changed it to reflect my condition as God ordained it to be. A small squeaky voice came from a freckled frail looking woman in front of me saying,

> "But you are alive and well Naomi, and that means you are yet blessed."

I replied sharply,

> "No I am not, I'd rather be dead and buried in my grave than be without my darling Elimelech and my two sons."

I was filled with uncontrollable emotions. I knew I needed to leave and hurry off to my house. I grabbed Ruth by the hand and pressed through the crowd that had assembled filled with the woman of the town.

Ruth and I went to my home where I lived before leaving Bethlehem. After getting comfortable and cleaning up, we sat and made small talk. Ruth volunteered to go out to the fields the following morning to start earning money for our living expenses. She told me that I was too old to have such a concern. I loved my daughter in law so much. She always put her own cares aside for others.

The following morning I heard a knock at the door. It was Boaz, a male relative of my husband. He was standing there shaking his head with a grand smile of welcome on his face. "Naomi, it is so good to see you", he greeted me with a soft kiss to my forehead. He stood there with such a strong countenance and authority in the clothing of wealth which he wore so fitly. He resembled Elimelech so much it was painful to look at him. I invited him inside where we sat at the breakfast table and talked.

I learned quickly that distance can make you forget what you have a right to at home. After breakfast, Boaz mentioned that he noticed the Moabite woman working in the fields. He had this big smile on his face. He had learned that she was my daughter-in-law. He said he could tell her love for me and her love for our God as she worked so diligently. I told him that she was precious to me and that God had to have truly sent her to our family. He told me that he had grace in his heart for her and that God let him know to show her favor. That made my heart so happy. I could not wait until she returned from the fields. He also told me that he had changed her working space to be directly in his view with his hand maidens. I told him how much I appreciated the kindness shown to Ruth and all the favor granted to her. Boaz stopped me in mid sentence and asked how I was doing? I told him I was empty, and I had returned to my homeland destitute, and that I would probably have to sell my husband's land of inheritance in order to survive.

Boaz reached across the table and gently took my hands and whispered, "You do remember the law of the Kinsmen Redeemer, don't you?" I told him to please refresh my weary memory. Boaz reminded me that there were two kinsmen redeemers left in my husband's family. I was so consumed in my grief, I had forgotten all about the kinsmen redeemer law that our culture and custom upheld concerning widowers and land. There were men left in my family and they were my husbands' brothers.

BOAZ EXPLAINS:

Naomi, when a man in our custom dies without leaving any heirs to his wife, it creates two problems. First, it endangers the family's inheritance, because if the widow remarried outside the family, the inheritance would go to her new family. The law accommodates these issues through a practice called the "Levirate Marriage," which means, a deceased man's brother or nearest relative is to marry the man's widow and father an heir thereby, being the one that could buy the land. The child would be considered the child of the deceased man, not of the biological father.

You may purchase the land back through the male relative or the Kinsmen Redeemer when you are financially able to or when the time of Jubilee returns, it will come back to you anyway. Ruth is now in a position to provide an heir for the continuance of your family's name. Then you will be able to nurse the kinsmen child as your very own son.

Before Boaz left, he informed me that he would find the other brother to my husband and offer the Levirate Marriage to him as it is his first right of refusal being the older. Boaz said if he refused, he would gladly accept both buying the land and marrying Ruth. I could not hold back the tears that were springing up like a living well inside of me. Could I truly be hearing correctly? All the hope and all the joy that filled me could not be contained.

When he left my presence, I had to sit down quietly and ponder the things of God and the navigation of His hands. God had redeemed me and restored me in a matter of hours of my being back home. I had no idea what God had in store for my future. I thought my future was over quite frankly. I rejoiced in my house with gladness. I rejoiced for Ruth and what she was about to come into. I had wished so badly to be able give her another son, and God made the impossible, possible through the Kinsmen Redeemer law. I didn't know who the other relative was, but I began to cry out to God, "please let the kinsmen redeemer be none other than Boaz, your servant". I danced and I shouted. I thought on the fact that I tried to convince Ruth to actually go back home to her people empty handed. Suddenly, it dawned on me that I could not remember the last time I had prayed to God. Silence came over me. I realized that I had not prayed to Him since the deaths of my sons. My praise and shouting transformed into me kneeling down before God repenting and asking His forgiveness for all the hatred and anger I had toward Him. I cried unto Him from my heart, I could feel His love fill my heart as I reached up toward heaven worshiping my sovereign God. My day was even more of a blessing because I was back with my God.

From that day on, I taught Ruth how to carry herself around Boaz and how to minister to him like no other woman could. God answered my prayer, the first brother to Elimelech refused to purchase the land and refused to marry Ruth because it would jeopardize his own inheritance. Also word got out that it also weighed on the fact that she was a Moabite. So, the option went to Boaz and he joyfully accepted. I wept with praise for weeks of the coming union of Boaz to Ruth. They married and had their first son who they named Obed. Over the years Obed begot Jessie, and Jessie begot King David whose throne the Savior and Messiah would sit upon according to the Prophets. Yes, none other than the King of Kings and the Lord of Lords who will forever reign would come through my family line.

So if you are God's child and you are going through some losses and some things that don't make sense, hold on, child of God. He is not through with you yet. Take it from me, there is something great in store waiting for you in the near future. Trust God and His sovereignty because I have learned that He truly knows what's best for you and me. I had mourned, grieved and remained angry for seven long years, but by God's grace, and wonderful love He looked beyond my faults and saw all of my needs. He kept me alive, He kept directing me and then He chose to bless me beyond my imagination. He had a miracle waiting for me at the end of my season in Moab. There is a blessing at the end of your Moab too. I would like to pass on to you, that God can certainly handle your human anger and confusion about what is happening in your life and all the "why's" that we ask God. He can handle your turning your back on Him at night before you go to sleep without saying your prayers, and waking up and not speaking to Him. But please don't test the hand of the living God for long. He loves you and He knows what's best for you. He has not forgotten you, nor has He forsaken you as we sometimes feel in our humanity. Yes, it was time for my husband to leave and my two sons left me too, but God never did and He never will. I will join my family again one day in heaven and we will all rejoice and praise our God.

* * * * *

CHAPTER 2
NAOMI, WHO ARE YOU MAD AT?
SELAH, PAUSE, LET'S DISCUSS

I lift my hat off to Naomi for so many reasons. She is a woman of God and a woman of integrity. In the midst of her matriarchal status, she dared to let her true pain and anger be known. A trait that we would all do well to learn. She didn't expose her pain in the privacy of her own home, but openly displayed her anger, grief and lowliness in front of her people. Naomi did not hold up any pretenses about the tragedies that happened back in Moab, nor did she try to appear to be something that she wasn't. In being real about where she was emotionally, spiritually, and psychologically, she demonstrated a strong healthy pattern of not suppressing her feelings like many people ordinarily do. The fact was that she wasn't happy, she was angry. She wasn't revengeful, she was angry. She wasn't covetous, she was simply angry. With whom was she angry? The Bible is clear that she was angry with four people. The first one was her husband who died and left her in Moab, the other two were her sons which she birthed who having died also left her in Moab. She was left in a foreign land among foreign people and foreign gods. Then her status went down. Her financial stability was threatened too, with no men to work in the fields. Her status was diminished from being a wealthy wife, well provided for to a wailing widow returning home with nothing to show for the years spent away. Lastly, she was most angry at God whom she felt had the power to prevent the travesties she experienced. She was so angry toward God. She didn't try to hide it, and she didn't try to camoflouge it. She made no excuses about her issues between her and her God. She would have to reckon with God and she did.

In the midst of her bitterness, she witnessed the sovereign God still at work in her life in spite of her professed anger toward Him. She saw that her anger toward God did not cut off the mercy and grace that He extended to her. Have you ever stopped talking to God because of your anger toward Him? Have you ever blamed God for pains, heartaches and let downs that you may have experienced or are currently experiencing in your life? What has God allowed to happen to you that has caused a strain in your relationship with Him?

*Is it the death of a loved one. *Is it the absence of a spouse that you have been waiting to return? *Is it the death of a parent? *Is it a disease which you have been stricken? *Is it financial difficulty? *Is it a certain career that you have been trying hard to get into but can't seem to meet the necessary requirements? *Is it a miscarriage from trying to have a baby? *Is it a parent's care that you long for as a result of an adoption when you were young? *Is it a young child that you lost due to sickness, or a senseless murder? *Is it the embarrassment of breaking off your engagement? *Is it the infidelity of your spouse or fiancee' resulting in him or her leaving you for another? *Is it being molested, raped, or beaten and you feel God could have stopped it and He didn't? Who are you mad at? What are you mad about? What is the source of your anger?

Throughout biblical accounts, humanity has questioned God's sovereignty from Abraham to Moses, from Rachael to Mary, the mother of Jesus. Job questioned God out of his pain, grief, anger, and confusion after he lost all of his children, his wealth, the respect of his wife, all his cattle and land, and his perfect bill of health. I am sure in Job's humanity, he must have gotten a little bitter. We hear him saying in Job 3:1-3, and 11-12.

> Job opened his mouth, and cursed his day. And Job spake, and said "Let the day perish on which I was born, and the night in which it was said, there is a man child conceived. Why did I not die from the womb? Why did I not give up the ghost when I came out of the womb? Why did the knees receive me? Or why the breast that I should suck."

After Job questioned himself and God, Job came to the revelation of the Sovereignty of God. He discovered that God does what He wants to do without getting anyone's permission. That's what Sovereignty is. After learning this lesson, Job had to conclude by saying:

"The Lord giveth and the Lord taketh away. Blessed be the name of the Lord."

Job finally understood that there is an appointed time unto man to be born and to die. It's an appointed time, which means it's God's time. Death is never timely with us and we can never prepare for it.

Naomi could not imagine that she still had great blessings coming to her even after losing three precious gifts. Though she felt abandoned, she would soon be full again and restored. She was sad that she didn't have anymore sons to give to her daughter-in-law, but the providence of God had already gone before her and prepared a blessing in the Kinsmen Redeemer that would allow her to have the fruit of her husband.

God acts as our Kinsmen Redeemer through his Son Jesus Christ when we suffer the loss of loved ones too. Jesus says to us, that "I will never leave you nor forsake you." Hebrew 13:5. He understands the pain of our longing for the presence of loved ones passed on. When we let Him into our hearts, His presence sufficiently fills those voids in our lives with His unconditional love, mercy and grace. Jesus understands being left and He also understands abandonment issues. Jesus wants to love us through our losses and through our loved ones' absences. We also read in scripture during the last few years of Jesus' ministry that those that had benefitted from Him the most, were suddenly abandoning Him. Yes, those that He healed, fed, and set free, abandoned Him. So many people in His life had left Him, that He turned to His disciples asking them "Will you too leave me?" Then we see in scripture where His own earthly father is absent at the scene of the cross. When we see Jesus hanging on the cross, we find only a few familiar friends and family members in the crowd that stayed until the end. However, Joseph, His earthly father was not there. Therefore we read with great comfort, the Hebrew account wherein it says:

"We do not have a high priest that cannot be touched with the feelings of our infirmities, but was in all points tempted like we were." Heb. 4:14-16.

In other words the pain you and I feel, He feels. He can sympathize and empathize with us, because He too experienced pain, disappointments, and let downs in this world.

We say that God is sovereign with great joy, but when it crosses the boundaries of our loved ones and comfort zones, His sovereignty becomes a thorn in our flesh. We then want God's sovereignty to always be in favor of our expectations, and if not, we tend to fall out with Him.

A servant once offered this parable:

> "We are all thine. When God is good and ready for us; He will bring us home. He has loaned us to the earth for a season, for some, seasons are long, for others, it's but a moment, but the gift of life is to be cherished and not offended by the legacy of anger and hatred toward God, but the praise and worship of His giving of His creature for that season. For one day, we too must return to the dust to live with him in Glory." /cyc

My sisters and brothers, do not let the losses in your life prevent you from going forward to the blessings that are waiting for you. God loves you with an everlasting love, and you have to trust that He knows what's best for you. We have to trust God and hope the eternal best for our deceased loved ones. They are spending eternity with our loving God. I encourage you today, if you are mad at God, humble yourself before Him and ask His forgiveness as Naomi did. Then, let Him heal your heart, because He is not mad at you. He stands waiting patiently to fill you with His love and great peace and to bring you into the fullness of your joy in Him.

CHAPTER 2
NAOMI, WHO ARE YOU MAD AT?
Q&A'S

(You may choose more than one answer)

1. Why was Naomi angry?
   a) She didn't want to walk back to Bethlehem
   b) She lost her husband and two sons
   c) She couldn't find another husband
   d) She was aging
   e) All of the above
   f) Other:______________________________

2. With whom was Naomi angry?
   a) Her husband
   b) Her daughters in law
   c) Her sons
   d) Her God
   e) All of the above
   f) Other:________________________________

3. Why did she change her name from Naomi to Mara?
   a) She was angry with God
   b) Because she suffered
   c) She like the name better
   d) Other:________________________________

4. How did the deaths of Naomi's husband and children reshape the way she saw herself?
   a) Fruitful
   b) Empty
   c) Failure
   d) All of the above
   e) Other:________________________________

5. Can we ever be fully prepared for death?

6. Have you ever lost a loved one?

7. Did you blame the loss of that loved one on God? If so, why?

8. Have you ever been angry at God for any reason?

9. Have you ever blamed your adverse conditions on God?

10. Did you know that we have the potential to get angry with God?

11. Have you ever admitted to being angry with God?

12. Who do you believe is responsible for our losses and traumas?
    a) Satan
    b) God
    c) We are
    d) A combination of all
    e) Other:________________________________

13. If you answered yes to the previous questions, are you still angry with God?

14. Define the sovereignty of God as it appears in the story:

15. How do we resolve our anger with God?
    a) Ask for his forgiveness
    b) Confess it
    c) Receive his restoring power
    d) Accept that God knows what's best
    e) Other:____________________________________

16. Boaz was the Kinsmen Redeemer in the lives of Naomi and Ruth who allowed them a new beginning. Who stands as our Kinsmen Redeemer in the midst of our losses, famines, and misfortunes?
a) Jesus Christ
b) Government
c) Our jobs
d) Our parents
e) Other:______________________________

How does the bible describe the Sovereignty of God in Proverbs 21:1?

____

According to Job 1:1-21 how does job experience God's Sovereignty?

____

____

CHAPTER 3
TAKE YOUR LAST BOW!

Luke 13:11-13 (KJV)

11) And behold there was a woman who had a spirit of infirmity eighteen years, and was bowed together and could in no wise lift up herself.

12) And when Jesus saw her he called her to him, and said unto her, Woman, thou art loosed from thine infirmity.

13) And he laid his hands on her; and immediately she was made straight, and glorified God".

***

The "Bent-over Woman" is the legendary name I was called for 18 long years. My real name is Doris. By the time I was 18 years old, my body was fully bent over to the point where I could not physically straighten up.

I was what you would call the black sheep in the family. I wasn't like anyone else, and I paid a high price for being different. For years, I thought I was created to be everyone's personal dart board for lashing out the most hideous words and painful names that anyone could think.

It all started when I first heard my mother say to her girlfriend Gayle that she didn't know what happened to me when I was born, and why I came out so differently. Then I heard her girlfriend return a comment asking her if she was sure that the doctors' gave her the right child, referring to me. I guess they didn't know that at the young age of four, I could understand every word they were saying. Momma laughed with her girlfriend, and she never knew I overheard that conversation to this day. That day planted a seed of feeling displaced in my heart that I shall never forget.

While growing older, I too wondered whether or not I was given to the right parents. I didn't resemble not one sister or brother. You see, I had a slight deformity. My skin was spotted with patches of dark and light marks, my nose was too wide, and my ears poked out. My sisters and brothers were very thin and light skinned like my mother and father. On top of that, I stuttered and couldn't speak as well as my sisters and brothers. They were ashamed of me and would make fun of my speech impediment. When they talked to me, they would pretend that they were stuttering. When we were at school, they introduced me by saying this is our weird sister who doesn't speak well.

During the times we played outside, my sisters and brothers didn't seem to want me around because they said I was too slow. I guess I was kind of young and only got in the way. After being ignored and rejected, I stayed in the house while my sisters and brothers played together. My brothers would tease me, calling me the slow ugly duckling out of the pond. "Go back in your pond", they would scream! I would run back into the house to my bedroom and rock myself while covering my ears. I didn't want to hear them, but the thoughts in my head still echoed in my mind. The words hurt so much, I couldn't make them go away.

My father really didn't have anything nice to say about me like he did when he spoke of my sisters and brothers. I will never forget, one summer daddy had arranged for a family portrait and "forgot" to ask me to come sit for it. I was still in my bedroom, and they never asked me to come downstairs for the painting.

From that day on, I stayed far away when they were doing family things to avoid blatant rejection. I thought to myself I was ugly and that was just a reality that I had to accept. I didn't know why God was punishing me. I would ask myself, "why did he make me to look this way?" I began to believe I was ugly like my brothers and the other children in school began to tell me. Then the name calling progressed to kids doing physical things like forcing me to act like certain animals in front of everyone. This only reminded me of how much I was hated by everyone, but I played along with it anyway. To win friends, I allowed myself to be the brunt of everyones' jokes and I ended up laughing at myself to keep the "security" of my "friendships." I would answer to whatever name they decided to call me. I would bow down to it, as I bowed down to imitating the animal noises they asked me to do. That was the best way I could describe what I allowed those kids to do to me. I would even give my allowance to whomever needed it. I didn't mind, because it won me friends that I otherwise wouldn't have had. Out of all the people that I bought to be my friend, I can honestly say I did have one true friend throughout every school season, Sheila Mackenberry.

She walked with a limp because one of her legs was shorter than the other. She would always tell me not to bow down to those horrible acts, she would rather be alone, but I wanted so badly to fit in. Sheila had a mother and father that loved her and even a baby brother that she got along with. I had neither.

As time went on, I developed medical problems that the doctors couldn't explain. After taking several blood tests and exams, they still didn't know what was wrong with me. My parents had to take me to the physician's office more often than they desired. Each time my body would become spasmatic with great pain, my parents seemed to grow more irritated with having to take off work and take me to the physicians office. I could feel their irritation. I regretted telling them I was in pain. I never knew what was medically wrong. The physicians would speak privately to my parents, and my parents would never tell me what was being said. All I knew was that I was given another prescription. This went on for years.

When I finally turned 18, I was so ready to move out and into an apartment with the only real friend I knew, Sheila Mackenberry. After I moved away from home, I noticed I was still lonely, empty and sad inside. I was so glad that I was no longer living at home where I felt like a burden to everyone, but I still wasn't at peace with myself.

Sheila noticed how sad I was around the house and asked what was wrong. I told her I was a little bothered with some things from my past. After listening to me, she suggested that I probably needed to resolve the struggles directly with my parents. I had not told Sheila everything about my childhood, she just knew that I was unhappy at home. I took her advice and decided to finally go talk with my parents. I contacted my mother and told her that I was coming over for dinner at the end of the week. I was so nervous for those three days leading up to the dinner, I couldn't eat or sleep.

Mother was always a chef at heart. Her cooking was the best. That was the only good memory that I had as a child. After we cleared the dishes from the table, I asked my parents if we could sit down and talk. They looked surprised, but were more than willing. During dinner, we made small talk.

They talked about my sisters and brothers successful careers and then asked when was I going to decide what I wanted to do with my life.

I ignored the question, because it was really too painful to answer. I didn't know what I wanted to be. My father interrupted my mother noticing the uneasiness that I was feeling. He asked what was on my mind. I started by asking them why they never treated me nice like they treated my sisters and brothers. I will never forget the astonished look on both of their faces. Then I asked why they didn't seem to love me as much as they loved my sisters and brothers. They were speechless. They glanced at one another then dropped their heads. I was still so nervous, but I took advantage of their silence to ask even more questions. I asked them why I.was never told I love you. "We do", they said almost in unison. I continued asking my questions, "Why was I never told what was medically wrong with me?" My mother started clearing her throat, coughing and fidgeted in her seat. I could tell she was getting uncomfortable, I just didn't know why. I went on telling them how miserable and traumatic my childhood had been. I told them that there was not one day of my life that had passed, when I wasn't laughed at or the object of somebody's jokes including my own family members. "Why?" I simply asked. I didn't realize how emotional I had gotten until I heard my voice crack. My mother had tears in her eyes. My father kept his head down looking at the table. I was not trying to start trouble, or make them feel bad, I just needed to know what was so wrong with me, why no one wanted to have anything to do with me.

Clearing his throat, my father began explaining a tragic incident 18 years ago. My mother was alone one morning. He was at work, and the other kids were at school. A man broke into our house and raped my mother. Nobody ever knew except for my father and my sisters and brothers. I felt so bad for my mother. I couldn't believe what I was hearing. As a result of the rape, she became pregnant and discovered later she was infected with a sexually transmitted disease. That disease transmitted to the child. My father took a deep breath and then said, "you are that child". "What do you mean Dad?" I screamed. "You are the baby that your mother was impregnated with by the rapist, Doris." In that split second, I thought I was loosing my mind. My head felt light. I stood up immediately. I remembered thinking, how could they keep this away from me all these years? Why did they let me live? I stood there watching their solemn faces drop down in their laps. I couldn't do anything. I could not even speak. My body felt paralyzed. My voice was gone. My parents were apologizing while I stood their crying. They wanted to hold me after all those years of rejecting me. Shaking my head no, I backed up not wanting them to touch me. I had to go. I ran out of the house, while hearing my parents begging me to come back. I ran all the way home. I tried to run away from the horrible news. I wished it was a bad dream and I would wake up.

The crying lasted for days, and then weeks. There were times I would wake up and my face would be wet from crying in my sleep. Sheila would come to my bedside many nights and pray for me. I would push her away not being able to accept the prayers for the resentment and pain I suffered. She would ask me to go to the temple with her, I refused each time. I couldn't even stand up from the burden of the pain that racked deep within my soul for years. I only went out for necessities, but never socially. The pain I lived with concerning the knowledge I had learned about myself caused me too much pain to deal with society.

After yeras of depression, I finally concluded that I didn't want to go on through life with this senseless pain. One morning, after my roommate left for work, I went to the kitchen to get a knife. I cut my wrist without hesitation and collapsed to the floor. As I laid in a fetal position, rocking back and forth hoping to die, several thoughts brought me peace. I would no longer have to suffer from the shame of my past, or badgering words from family and friends, or laughter in my face, or being sick with an incurrable sexual disease or trying to find someone to love me and accept me. While I laid there, I could feel the cold and the darkness creep into the room. I could feel myself drifting, growing weak. But in the distance of my mind, I could hear a voice whisper "hold on, the pain is only temporary." The next thing I knew, I was being brought to consciousness by Sheila, my roommate.

SHEILA SPEAKS:

Finding Doris that morning was the most devastating experience I ever had in my life. I was so glad that I forgot my coat and decided to come back home to get it, otherwise, she would have died in that puddle of blood.

When she was released from the physicians care facility, I brought her home and cared for her as my own sister.

I knew about the depression and pain of her past that was tormenting her every day, but there was nothing I could do, but pray. Her suicide attempt didn't come as a total shock. It was so hard to believe all the emotional pain that she had suffered all those years. Quite frankly, it was amazing to me that she did not try to kill herself before. I never realized how crippling words could be and how one's self-worth could just dissipate into thin air. I tried to reaffirm her beauty and significance throughout our friendship. I made a point of staying by her side, encouraging her everyday. I told her that I loved her like the sister I never had, and that I was so glad God brought her into my life. I knew Doris was my assignment from God. Many people chastised me for spending to much of my life helping my friend, but I knew God sent her to me to care for. Doris was so smart and gifted, I could not understand why anyone would maliciously hurt such a sweet and giving person. Doris' only aspirations and ambitions in life were to become accepted and loved. She disconnected herself from her entire family, so I assured her that I would be her family and would never hurt her. Doris experienced years of depression because of her past. She walked bent over as if she was carrying the entire world on her back. In a sense, I guess you could say that she was carrying many things on her back, because she could not let the truth of her past go.

One morning, Doris finally accepted my offer of years inviting her to worship with me. I will never forget that day. Now, I will let her tell you about that day.

DORIS SPEAKS:

Sheila had been trying to get me to go to the temple service with her ever since we became roommates. I would always tell her not this week, maybe next time. After years of emotional pain, depression and feeling worthless, I woke up one Sabbath wanting to go to temple service with her. Of course, Sheila was shocked at my readiness when she was about to walk out the door. I told her that I wanted to hear some good news, if there was some to be heard.

Every time Sheila came home from worship, she was always in a good mood, and I wanted that same feeling. I didn't know what to expect, as we took our seats in the back of the temple. A few people turned around to see who had just come in. The Rabbi that was teaching stopped. He seemed to be looking directly to the back right where Sheila and I sat. I was so tired from the walk, but I could not help but feel his piercing eyes staring at me. It felt as if he was looking directly into my soul. I thought could he actually see me from way up there in the back of the room? Women were separated from the men, but I could still hear and see what was going on. Suddenly, the Rabbi said "Come here". He did not call out anyone's name, but I found myself responding to his call. Somehow, I believed he was talking to me. Before I knew it, I stood up without thinking or caring, and I began walking toward him. It would be a long walk, but I was on my way. I heard inquisitive whispers from the anxious audience wondering why the Rabbi stopped teaching. I blocked everyone out of my mind and focused on him as I continued to walk. Feelings of joy started leaping inside of me Who is this man? I wondered. Then as I was getting closer to him, that distant voice I heard as I laid on the floor the day I tried to commit suicide, saying "the pain is only temporary" tears began to roll down my face. They were not tears of pain like before, but tears of overwhelming peace and excitement. I could barely keep focus because of my condition and the tears clouding my vision, but I finally made it to him.

Now, I was standing right in front of him. He slowly kneeled down and looked me right in my eyes. With a resounding tone, he said, "Woman, thou art loosed from thine infirmities." Immediately, a wave of heat ran through my body. As he raised up taking me by my hand, we stood up together. Before I knew it, I was standing straight, tall, and strong. I was now standing face to face, eye to eye with the man that compelled me to come to him. I lifted up both my arms unto heaven my head went back, and I screamed at the top of my voice "Glory to God." I could hear Sheila in the background screaming praises to God saying, "Hallelujah." I didn't know I knew how to praise Him, but somehow I did. My arms didn't want to come down from reaching toward heaven. My body was straight now! Every second I thought about it, I jumped and shouted the

Glory of God. I screamed over and over again shouting Hallelujah! The Rabbi just touched me and spoke those life changing words into my spirit. He said I was loosed from my infirmities. I will never forget those words. Folks were starting to get irritated around me, but I didn't care. And when Jesus touches you, you won't care what folk say about you either. You will just praise Him until you can't praise him anymore. I have been praising Him from that day on. The Messiah saw me and called me to Himself. When He caused me to stand up, every dead thing inside of me stood up. My life stood up, my dignity stood up, my pride stood up, my femininity stood up, my significance stood up, my joy and praise stood up in me and was loosed to go free.

Chapter 3
TAKE YOUR LAST BOW
SELAH! PAUSE, LIFE LESSONS

When Jesus knew that Doris was present in her solemn condition and searching soul, it stopped Him in His teaching tracks. She changed His environment. He could not utter another word until He healed this bowed down woman from her infirmities. She touched the emotions and heart of the loving Savior so much so, that He called her without addressing her by name. The power of His petition was so direct and clear that He compelled Doris's spirit to come forth. His love begged for her, His sensitivity begged for her, and His healing power waited patiently for her to reach her final destination that would change her life forever!

He spoke words into her body that she had never heard before from anyone. Words of Life. Words of love, peace, and great hope. His words cancelled every judgement of old, every laughter and ridicule directed to her and every deadly pronouncement of failure and insignificance. Jesus healed her! He healed her mind. He healed her thoughts and caused her to have new ones. Then He touched her body and caused the elaciticity that had turned hard and cold in her body to return to its natural posture. He caused her to stand up straight in the face of the devil's scheme to destroy her. He ordained her to never be bowed down again. No wonder she could not help but praise and shout to the Glory of God, she was LOOSED! What was she loosed from? She was loosed from years of despair and hopelessness. She was loosed from confusion and discouragement. She was loosed from low-self esteem and whatever else that caused her life to be filled with darkness and depression. Then He loosed her to be free, to love, to dream, and to believe and hope again. She was loosed to stand in the power of God and walk in His promises.

When Doris found out the painful knowledge about the raping of her mother, and her true biological father, it literally crippled her causing her to be bent over in emotional and physical pain for 18 long years. She was bent over by shame, rejection, and deception, but thanks be to God for revealing His truth to Doris that day. He told her His truth which put her past to an open shame. She learned that she was loved and accepted in the Godhead bodily before she was in her mother's womb. God loved her. She learned that God would give her beauty for her ashes, the oil of joy for her mourning, and the garment of praise for the spirit of her heaviness! God loved her. She learned she was created in the image and the likeness of God. She could not speak well, but God loosed her stammering tongue and caused her to prophesy the Truth of God Almighty with clarity and boldness. She learned that her spiritual father declared through His prophets " I know the thoughts I think toward you, saith the Lord, thoughts of peace, and not of evil, to give you an expected end and a hope (Jeremiah 29:11). Doris walked away that day free in Jesus embracing the love of God.

The old nursery rhyme that says, "sticks and stones may break my bones, but WORDS will never hurt me", this is a lie from the devil. Words do hurt, words do injure, and sometimes they hurt more than sticks and more than stones. I have personally witnessed and have also been subjected to destructive and demeaning words directed to me. We often underestimate the lasting impact and impressions of words spoken in mid air. Often words are taken for granted and minimized, but just as bullets are shot into the air, when they come down they can easily kill you. I've heard husbands and wives say to one another after a heated argument, "Oh you know I didn't really mean what I said," failing to realize the power and damage already inflicted by that critical word spoken in a moment of anger. I have heard parents curse out their children and call them hideous names that will travel with them all the days of their lives and shape their perceptions about themselves. I have also witnessed employers calling their employees stupid, incompetent, watching their self-esteem crumble in the midst of their career. Once words are planted into the hearing, it starts the process of internalization. They can't just automatically be revoked because of a timely apology. Words run their course and establish their grounds in your being. Words are so powerful, and if the truth be told, words can have you bent over for 18 long years just like Doris.

Where is the bent over woman today who is bound by words, evil deeds, sickness, a shameful past and hopeless future? Wherever you are today, the Omniscient Savior stops in His tracks for you. He sees you right where you are, and He beckons for you to come to Him, just as He did the bent over woman. He wants to undo what Satan has done to you. He wants to loose you of whatever has you bound today. He stands at the door of your life saying "Come here". Where? Into His love. Where? Into His acceptance and to His mercy. Where? To the good plan He has for your life and not evil. Where? To hear His thoughts concerning you and how much you are loved already. Where? To the secret place of the most high God, and under the shadows of the Almighty to be covered by His grace and mercy forever. Where? To the assembly of the Lord, to worship Him openly on the housetops and in His temples? Where? To a place in your spirit that will consume you with His overwhelming perfect peace and His abundant joy that will give you life and life more abundantly. It was for this cause that He came into the world just for you and me. He says in Matthew 9:12: They that be whole need not a physician, but they that are sick. How do we rid our minds from these hideous words, names, and labels that have been planted in our minds throughout the years? We exchange them. Thank God, we have the two-edged sword which is the Word of God as our weapon that will combat every word of the enemy that he uses in the form of a fiery dart to destroy us. We can uproot his words with God's Word which is the absolute truth of how we are seen in God's eyes. The Word of God is given to us so that we can walk in the power and authority and the truth of God. Why? because the devils weapons are <u>words</u> and <u>thoughts</u> that he tries to plant in our minds to bring us into fear, doubt, discouragement, and destruction. That's why we are instructed to defeat the negative words imposed by tongues of men in II Corinthians 10:4-5 the Apostle Paul encourages us that: "The Weapons of our warfare (that which we fight with and struggle with) are not carnal (natural) but mighty (supernatural) through God to the pulling down of strongholds); casting down imaginations, and every high thing that exalteth itself against the knowledge of God (the Word of God), and bringing into captivity (arresting it and put it in a line up against the Word of God) every thought (every word) to the obedience of Christ (the power of Christ)."

Then we are given, Isaiah 54:17 which tells the child of God that: "No weapon that is formed against us shall prosper; and every tongue that shall rise against us in judgment THOU shalt condemn. This is the heritage of the servants of the Lord, and their righteousness is of me, saith the Lord."

Remember, when the Devil begins to tell you things that are contrary to the Word of God, you condemn it immediately and confess the promised Word over your life and keep standing tall in Jesus Name!

Chapter 3
TAKE YOUR LAST BOW
Q&A'S

(You may have more than one answer)

1.Doris was raised around what type of environment?
a) Demeaning
b) Judgmental
c) Healthy
d) Destructive
e) Other:______________________________

2.Doris' family made her feel
a) Very close
b) Important
c) Like an outcast
d) Special
e) Other:______________________________

3.Doris was a very
a) Timid girl
b) Ashamed girl
c) Angry girl
d) Sad girl
e) Other:______________________________

4.In school, Doris had many friends
a) No
b) Yes
c) One
d)Other:______________________________

5.Doris' perception of God as it relates to her life was:
a) Special
b) Bewildered
c) Non-trusting
d) Confusing
e) Other:______________________________

6. How did Doris gain friends?
a) Bought them with money and favors
b) Attracted them automatically
c) Gave them her lunch
d) Begged for friendship
e) Other:______________________________

7.What was medically wrong with Doris?
a) Pregnant
b) She had AIDS
c) She had a sexually transmitted disease
d) Nothing, she had a clean bill of health
e) Other:_______________________________

8. Did she receive love from her father
a) No
b) Yes
c) Sometimes
d) Other:______________________________

9. Do you have any secrets that would impact your family negatively?

10. What makes us keep secrets?
a) Anger
b) Revenge
c) Shame
d) Fear
e) Other:________________________________

11.Who suffers the most from our secrets

a) Our family

b) Ourselves

c) Everyone

d) Other:______________________________

12. What did Doris desire in her adulthood

a) Family

b) Real love

c) Dreams

e) Other:________________________________

13. What was Doris' solution to finally having peace

a) Attempting to commit suicide

b) Drink

c) Jog

d) Watch television

e)Other:________________________________

14. What harm do secrets cause in family situations
a) Create distrust
b) Create anger and rage
c) Create a void of love
d) It creates mental and spiritual bondage
e) All of the above
f) Other:______________________________

15. Should you have secrets in your family?
Yes or No, please discuss.

According to Matthew 11:28-30 what does Jesus offer for those of us that have been burdened down and tired of lifes'

____

____

According to Luke 4:18 why was Jesus sent?

____

____

According to II Corinthians 10: 4 & 5 how do we combat negative words that bombared our thoughts and attempt to shape us and mold our self-esteem?

____

____

____

According to Ephesians 4:29 what are we admonished to refrain from?

____

____

CHAPTER 4
THE GENERATIONAL BATON
(Luke 8:1-2)

> 1) And it came to pass after ward, that He went throughout every city and village, preaching and bringing the glad tidings of the kingdom of God; and the twelve were with Him,
>
> 2)And certain women, which had been healed of evil spirits and infirmities, Mary called Magdalene out of whom went seven devils.

***

My name is Mary called Magdalene. My biography is very short in scripture, therefore, allow me to fill in all the blanks for you.

My mother introduced my sisters and me to the very lucrative family business which had been passed down from generation to generation. This included training all the younger girls on how to be a sexual delicatessen for a small price. My mother had clients from all over the countryside. All of her clients were married men. In fact, that was her criteria. It held some sort of security for everyone involved. As I'm sure you have guessed, my mother was a ringmaster of a harlots' house. This was one of the many generational curses in my family.

In my town, women made their living either in the fields or working in a harlot's house. Neither option was attractive to me. However, my family didn't offer me a choice. To make matters worse, there were no birth control or any male contraceptives in our day. So, we bore bastard babies by our tricks. No one ever married in my family. This was the second generational curse. Because all the babies born to my sisters and I were girls, the family business continued from one generation to the next. As long as there were girls being born, the harlot baton would carry on.

We were thoroughly trained by the age of nine years old. We dressed like women of the night in grown-up clothes. I wore tight clothes that revealed everything my body was and was not. My mother would not allow us to wear anything girly and youthful for fear that it would frighten our customers. I wore heavy eye makeup, lipstick, cheap perfumes, and high heels all day long. We learned how to seduce with our eyes and undress a man with our teeth. We were also trained to pick pocket a man with a simple handshake, while walking casually beside him. Clearly my life as a child was not like the other girls in my age group. I thought of nothing but to be a sex object for sex crazy men.

I didn't learn anything about love and being in love, because my mother taught us that men never really love women, they only pretend to love them. I overheard conversations from girls my age as they walked by our house. They talked about being in-love, and their dreams to get married and have a family. I wondered if they knew the real truth about men. I believed my mother, because all of the men we had to sleep with were married, weird and strange. I was asked to spank men with their own belts, so that they could get off. Once a client asked me to pretend that I was a patient coming to see an OB- GYN doctor, and he wanted to rape me. Another client wanted me to pretend as if I were his mother and then molest him. I personally liked the men who came in and wanted to be beaten. This gave me a chance to take out my true anger on them, and so I would beat them real good. They came in all different colors, sizes and shapes. Sometimes, I would think about their wives and how miserable they must have been with these low down dirty perverts that we had to entertain. As a growing child, and on into adulthood, I became a very angry person. To look at me you would never know. I hid it behind my seductive smile and my provocative walk because I always had to be "on" in case potential business was around. I was angry with everyone. I always asked the question, "Why was I born into this world? Why was I put in this world of freaks and perverts? Why couldn't I be like other little girls and do little girl things." I wanted my life and my body to be precious to just one person, but the more it was used the more those dreams seemed out of touch. I began to believe I could never ever be special to anyone. So I was stuck. Being stuck is painful, uncomfortable and frustrating. So I played my role for over 25 years just the way Momma taught us. I hated her at times and resented her weakness for not being strong enough in her generation to pull my sisters and me out of this whole horrid lifestyle. She didn't have to accept the baton, or did she? I remembered hoping for a way out, and saying I'm not going to have to do this all of my life. I thought perhaps a good man would come and steal me away, and then I could live a normal life. A man that would turn my hatred away from men and prove to me that all men were not dogs and unfaithful. I searched in every man I had to sleep with for a difference and a spark of hope. It seemed to never come. I guess I was looking in the wrong places.

One day I received the strangest request that ever walked in our doors on two feet. A tall blonde man walked in accompanied by a very attractive woman. The place immediately started buzzing, because we never had a woman visit our business before. Everyone was wondering what was going on. We learned that she was his wife. Even more shocking, his fantasy was to see his wife lay with another woman! My mother felt I was the better person for the job and therefore assigned this couple to me. I was nervous. I had never done anything like this. I thought, what would happen? I was scared, yet part of me was excited.

It seemed like an eternity as we climbed the stairs to my sex room. Once we were in the room, he told her to disrobe so that we could get started. Instead of disrobing, she broke into tears. He stormed out of the room in disgust and told her to get home the best way she could. I was shocked and did not know what to do with this crying woman in front of me. I felt obligated to comfort her. She was in so much pain. She tried several times to get herself together and stop crying, but as soon as she would, she would break down again. I kept holding her and stroking her dark beautiful hair. Finally, she was able to compose herself. I found out her name was Nia. She told me that her husband started bringing home pornographic material and insisted that she view them with him. He told her that it would enhance their love life, because he needed more stimulation. She said he broke her heart when he asked her to participate, because it said to her that she wasn't enough stimulation for him anymore after just three years of marriage. Nia told me that once she agreed to look at the materials with him, he started talking about having different sexual exercises in bed. Then she yelled, "This is the man that I forfeited my dreams and ambitions for so that he could become successful. Now he wants to reduce me down to a little sexual toy." I had never been faced with a situation like this and didn't know what to do with it. I started rubbing her shoulders as she rested in my arms. I could easily empathize with her over being misused and mistreated by a man. Unfortunately, she was married to hers, and I just had to service mine, but they too regarded me as a piece of meat. Her pain was my pain and the source of her pain was the same source as mine, sick men who did not love, nor show women any respect or honor. I held her tighter and closer to me telling her it was going to be alright. She hugged me back. Before we knew it, we lived out her husband's fantasy without his presence. It was incredible. I had never felt this connected with anyone before in my entire 25 years. The intimacy between us, I could not describe or believe existed between two people. That night my life changed. Nia and I saw each other at least once a week without her husband's knowledge. My mother thought we had just become good friends.

I later decided to save my own money, purchase my own house, and open a house for women only who needed compassion, intimacy, and comfort. The whole idea gave me such a since of pride and joy. I saw all the pro's and con's of course. The pro's being I would have a love that I never knew existed, and I could provide an avenue for women who desired to experience this ultimate companionship. In addition, I was stopping innocent baby girls from coming into my generational curse of harlotry. The cons' were, my mother would probably want to kill me, and my sisters and family would disown me. It was a price that I was glad and willing to pay because of the love I found in Nia. I concentrated on the pro's and the happiness I knew I would have in my new found lifestyle. I relished in the fact that my business would build women's self-esteem. I would provide women an opportunity to be nurtured, loved, receive affection, and continual affirmations of their sensuality and significance. I was empowered by the love I had for my new love, Nia, and how wonderful she said I made her feel. We were so happy together and she eventually left her husband.

Just months into the business, I began meeting women from all over the country that wanted to experience our services. Word of mouth is powerful. Married women and single women came from various backgrounds and painful places. Some had been molested, raped, beaten, divorced, and rejected from their husband.

I heard many reasons as to how women ended up on our doorsteps which often made me quite sad. I'll never forget one woman came and said she always preferred women over men from the day she was born. She said she never felt comfortable with a man not one day in her life. Then she concluded by saying God made her like that. I thought that to be pretty interesting. Out of all the madness I had lived through, even I knew God made man and woman for one another, no matter how strange the world was around me. However, I didn't argue with her because I too was accomplishing love the best way I could.

Then something unforseen happened. A young man came by the house one night wondering if I could direct him where he could go and be with another man. I told him no. I slammed the door in his face because of the hatred I held toward all men. I was not concerned whether or not he ever found love.

After years of managing an around-the-clock business and maintaining my relationship with Nia, I began to transform into a different type of person. I found myself being out of control of my ego, my sexuality, and my reasoning.

One day while attempting to be intimate with Nia, she yelled out "If I wanted a man, I would have stayed with my husband." She told me that I had changed and had become too aggressive. She said sometimes I scared her with my aggressive, wild actions. I was shocked. She said my ways were getting too masculine and rough. I knew the things that Nia said were true. I just didn't know what to do about it. I was desiring sexual encounters that I didn't understand. My sexual desire escalated to wanting sex everyday all day long. It felt like I was trapped in a world that I could not leave. I felt like a sex parasite with an insatiable hunger. I even found myself not being satisfied with the usual sexual pleasures that we participated in. There was a side of me that was itching to incorporate pain within our sexual encounters. I pinched and slapped Nia on certain parts of her body and enjoyed watching her cringe and say "ouch". I was out of control. There were times when I would get so lost in a night of wild sex that the next morning I literaly felt like something or someone was taking over my mind and body. I even had thoughts of suicide when my mind and body felt out of control while I was fully awake.

Months later, a woman came knocking very hard at my door. She was beautiful. I had never seen her before. I thought she was a potential client, but she was asking me to come outside with her. She was so pretty, I would have followed her anywhere. Grabbing my jacket, we walked out toward the streets. I noticed a crowd at the end of the roadside gathering around a man. Walking toward the crowd, I wondered what was going on this early in the afternoon. What was this man saying? He had a captivated audience. The people stood in awe at his speaking. Then I noticed that all the women who worked for me were in the crowd too.

What was this? Who was he? I thought to myself I was feeling a little apprehensive, but curious enough to keep going. The lady who came to the house grabbed me by the hands making her way through the crowd, pushing me right to this man. Looking at him, I didn't feel the instant hatred as I did every single man that I had previously come in contact with. It felt good in his presence, almost embarrased. I can't explain it.

The stranger looked upon me with a warm smile. I almost felt very uncomfortable with him. He spoke to me with Great Power saying "Mary, today Satan no longer has you bound, you are free! I command every seducing demon to come out of you! I loose you from the demon of lust that seeks to deceive you from the truth of God! I destroy the perverted demon that has attached himself to you! I demand the lesbian demon that has tried to overshadow you to be destroyed! I command the hatred demon to bow down to the power of the Love of God! I arrest the Masochistic demon to take flight from your body! And I cancel the suicidal demon who sought to take your life! BE FREE AND WALK IN NEWNESS OF LIFE!

I literally experienced an EXODUS of sin fleeing my body so rapidly that I was physically limp when he finished speaking to me. I realized then, he wasn't speaking to me, but that which held me bound. He was speaking to the spirit that controlled me. I had never remembered crying and rejoicing. But I could not help worshipping him. I was worshiping the Man of God. He commanded the demonic activity in my life to leave my body! Do you hear me? Who is this man that commands demons to flee and take flight at his very words? It's Jesus! Only Jesus. Only Jesus! Only Jesus! Only Jesus. Only Jesus!

Chapter 4
THE GENERATIONAL BATON
SELAH, PAUSE AND LET'S LEARN

Yes, only Jesus could free Mary from all the demonic activity that held her captive. Only Jesus could open the prison gates to her mind, body, and soul and cause her to go free. Only Jesus could forgive her sins and wash her whiter than snow. And only Jesus could snatch her out of the very gateway of hell and all of it's trenches.

Mary was deceived in many areas of her life, but her primary area when she met Jesus was lust and all of the ungodly behavior that fell under the umbrella of lust. As scripture states, the by product of lust includes: "hatred, jeaslousy, envy, covetousness, lasciviousness, homosexuality, uncleanliness, witchcraft, rapist, murderers, and like such were some of you, no ye not that any that do these things shall not inherit the kingdom of God". (1st Corin. 6:9). Lust comes from Satan. Lust is selfish and seeks its own gratification. Lust is in direct opposition to love and is often a counterfeit which is often mistaken for love. That's what Mary and Nia had. Because they were both lacking in the same areas of need (love, respect, honor, dignity, identity, and significance) they gravitated to each other believing it was love that they had found in each other. It was a set up from Satan. Satan preys on the voids and the innocent needs in our lives. He then presents us with a personalized counterfiet package, with a touch of perversion, sending it to our doorstep, signed, sealed, and delivered. How do you know if you are operating by God's will or Satan's will. Satan specializes in making you think the package is the right thing and the real thing. We must be careful with our feelings and emotions. The fact that it feels good, may taste good, may appear to be stable and dependable, safe and secure, and not hurting a soul, does not mean it is good in the eyes of God. And, if it goes against the will of God according to his Word, no matter how good it feels and how wonderful it seems, if it's not ordained by God, it's from Satan. That's one of Satan's more subtle attributes.

Lust came into the world when Satan was extricated from heaven. Since then, his plan is to interrupt God from reproducing Himself in humanity, through the family structure that God ordained (Husband and wife and children.) Therefore, Satan created same sex relationships to spite God and destroy His plan! This blatant, arrogant working of Lust caused God to destroy two entire cities called Sodom & Gomorrah. The wickedness and lewdness dominated the cities and the people therein. Sodom and Gommorah were known as sexual capitals promoting homosexuality in it's rawest sense. While many claimed to be sorely in love with one another, God severely judged that city to the end of destruction. (Genesis 19:29)

What do demons look like? What do they do? Demonic activity has typically been described and portrayed in our entertainment world as, unseen spirits, spooking flying ghosts, things that come out only on Halloween night, and people that are posssessed as actress Linda Blaire demonstrated in the movie "The Exorcist." This depiction is only a partial truth. Satanic activitiy in its entirety produces the negativism in human behavoir (i.e., hatred, murder, lying, cheating, etc.)

In Scripture, Jesus called certain religious people children of the devil when they denounced his Authority, Diety, Lordship and truth about a Holy God. The fact of the matter is, in this life we will serve either God or Satan. There is no middle ground. The Bible teaches us that we cannot serve two masters at the same time, we will either hate the one and love the other. Matthew 6:24. This is the most simplistic and practical picture of demonic expression and objective.

To further demonstrate the demonic presence amongst us, we must first grasp the nature by which they come:

> Demonic spirits evolved simply as a result of Satans' rebellion for a higher position against God. He and one-third of the angels were cast down from their heavenly place with God. Consequently, their primary mission then became to utterly destroy God's creation and perfect plan for humankind. They did this by enrobing themselves in flesh in order to destroy the destiny of humankind with his God.

This attempt to destroy God's plan for humankind is reflective in Satans' massive influence in the world with its' evil attacks. That's why the number of abortions is increasing. That's why child abuse is becoming a common occurence. That's why there are teenage killings and massive suicides. That's why incest of baby girls and boys, divorce, - adultery- homosexuality are all so prevalent in our world today. Satan seeks to turn the course of the natural wholesome world that God created, into an unnatural place of habitation where anything and everything goes. It is the unnatural, ungodly, unclean, inappropriate behavior that evidences the influence of demonic activity in our lives. Individuals that do these things are bound in demonic activity and need deliverance.

What has you bound today? What is it that won't let go of you? What is it that you struggle with that seems to have you out of control? What is it that you believe you can't break free from? Deliverance has already been provided for you. The power is available to break the strongholds of Satan's influence in your life. Please know that there is no bondage, no sin, no habit, no lifestye, and no demonic power that can hold you from the Omnipotent Savior. Understand that there is no wrong that He can't right; there is no dirt that He can't cleanse you from. There is no mindset that he cannot change. He didn't come to judge you, He came to justify you. He didn't come to label you, but to liberate you. He didn't come to sentence you, but to save you. He didn't come to ridicule you, but to receive you and redeem you by His blood that He shed for you. He didn't come to leave you, but to love you to himself.

Just as He came to Mary's street and delivered her from every demonic activity in her life, He stands today to do the same for you! Luke 4:18 reads:

> 18. The Spirit of the Lord is upon me, Because He has anointed me to preach the Gospel to the poor. He has sent me to proclaim release to the captives, and recovery of sight to the blind, to set free those who are downtrodden, to proclaim the favorable Year of the Lord.

If you want Jesus to come into your life today and destroy the demonic activity that you have been bound by, repeat this life changing prayer:

Dear Lord:
I repent and ask you to come into my heart and forgive my sins and give me eternal life. I believe that you gave yourself for my sins that you might deliver me from this present evil world and every demonic activity in my life. I believe that you love me and have washed me from my sins in your own blood. I believe that God raised you from the dead and I now accept you as my Lord and Savior. Please fill me with your precious Holy Spirit and teach me in all your ways. Amen.

My friend, know that God has heard your humble prayer and has answered you. You are no longer under the stronghold of Satan. You are now under the jurisdiction of God. You are GOD'S child. I welcome you into the family of God as you have just now been Born Again". I encourage you according to the scriptures as recorded in John 3:3, to unite in fellowship with other Bible-believing "Born Again" Christians where you will learn how to walk in Christ and maintain your deliverance. We are encouraged to study and learn of this new way of life as recorded in God's Word in I Peter 2:2, where it says, "As newborn babes, desire the sincere milk of the Word, that you may grow thereby."

Now, lest we be ignorant of Satan's devices, we who are already in Christ Jesus can be demonically oppressed. Notice, I didn't say, demonically possessed, because, when we accept Jesus, He comes in our lives and lives in us. We then become the house where the Holy Spirit resides. Therefore, Satan spends his time trying to oppress us as a result of being disobedient, thereby attempting to shame our God and destroy our witness. If you are going through demonic oppression and are struggling with strongholds of your flesh, repeat this prayer:

Dear Lord:
I confess my sins. I thank you that according to I John 1:9 you tell me if I confess my sins you are faithful and just to forgive me and cleanse me from all unrighteousness. Father I pray that you strengthen me. Open my eyes and show me the areas of my life that do not please you and grant me the strength, grace and wisdom to resist any sin or weight that would prevent our

fellowship. Work in me to cleanse me from all ground that would give the Devil a foothold. I resist the devil and draw near to you. I resist and denounce all familiar spirits. I resist and denounce all oppressive spirits. I resist and denounce all sexual sins that try to overcome. I destroy the strongholds of Satan formed against my will today. I give my will to you. Heavenly Father, and choose to make the right decision of faith. I thank you that you dwell in my body and you have caused my body to be the temple of the Holy Ghost (I Cor. 3:16-17; 1 Cor 6:19-20 . I cover myself with the Blood of the Lord Jesus Christ for both the new believers and the restored Christians. I set myself in agreement with you this day in Jesus Name! Continue to walk in the newness of life in Jesus Christ!

Chapter 4
THE GENERATIONAL BATON
Q&A'S

1. What was Mary's solution to stopping baby girls being born into the world?
   a) Contraceptives
   b) Lesbian relationshps
   c) Abortion
   d) None of the above
   e) Other:________________________

2. Did Mary have a choice in being a pre-teenage harlot?
   a) Yes
   b) No
   c) Other:_________________________

3. What were some of the characteristics of Mary's environment while growing up?
   a) Nurturing
   b) Healthy
   c) Perverted
   d) Dangerous
   e) Acceptable behavior
   f) Other:__________________________

4. Mary was trained to do what to the clients?
   a) Pick pocket
   b) Undress them with her teeth
   c) Tell bed time stories
   d) Entice them.
   e) Other:___________________________

5. What did Nia's husband want to do at the harlot's house?
a) Pray
b) Fulfill his fantasy with her and Mary having intimacy
c) Ejaculate in front of them
d) None of the above
e)Other:______________________________

6. Have you been exposed to pornogaphy?
a) Yes
b) No
c) Other:______________________________

7. If yes, how did you feel about it?

8. Ultimately, how did Mary feel in her new lesbian lifestyle?
a) Empowered by the women
b) Stupid
c) Confused
d) Still wanting more
e) Other:______________________________

9. Who were Mary's role models?
a) She did not have any
b) Her mother
c) Her father
d) Nia her lover
e) None of the above
d) Other:______________________________

10. How does God view same sex relationships in the book of Romans Chapter 1:18-32?
a) Natural
b) Unnatural
c) Right
d) Abomination against God
e) Other:______________________________

11. In God's word, how does one rid themselves of this type of lifestyle?
a) Repent and pray
b) Change their minds
c) Surrender to God
d) Acknowledge it is sin and against God
e) Renounce and release the demonic activity to the Lord
f) All of the above
g) Other:______________________________

12. Is there forgiveness for this type of sin?
a) Yes
b) No
c) Other:____________________________

13. Who defines love and relationships?
a) We do
b) God does
c) Dr. Feel good
d) Society
e) Other:____________________________

14) Where is homosexuality first mentioned in the bible?
a) Europe
b) Sodom and Gomorah
c) Egypt
d) Ceasaria
e) Genesis
f) Other:_____________________________

15. In your opinion, what is the difference between Lust and Love?

16. Pornography is
a) Against God
b) Sexual exploitation
c) A web of addictive immoral behavior
e) Other:___________________________

According to Exodus 20: 5&6 what are the conditions that God will extend his mercy and grace on a generational that hate him and disobeys him?

____

____

According to 1st John 1:9 what will God do for the sinner who confesses their sins?

____

____

CHAPTER 5
BEHOLD, THE 7TH MAN
St. John 4:1-29 (KJV)

4) And he must needs go through Samaria.
5) Then cometh he to a city of Samaria, which is called Sychar, near to the parcel of ground that Jacob gave to his son Joseph.
6) Now Jacob's well was there. Jesus therefore, being wearied with his journey, sat thus on the well; and it was about the sixth hour.
7) There cometh a woman of Samaria to draw water.
8) Jesus saith unto her, give me to drink. (For his disciples were gone away unto the city to buy meat.)
9) Then saith the woman of Samaria unto him, how is it that thou being a Jew, asketh drink of me, which am a woman of Samaria? For the Jews have no dealings with the Samaritans.
10) Jesus answered and said unto her, if thou knew the gift of God, and who it is that saith to thee, give me to drink, though wouldest have asked of him, and he would have given thee living water.
11) The woman saith unto him, Sir, thou has nothing to draw with, and the well is deep; from whence then hast thou that living water?
12) Art thou greater than our father Jacob which gave us the well, and drank thereof himself and his children, and his cattle.
13) Jesus answered and said unto her whosoever drinketh of this water shall thirst again. But whosoever drinketh of the water that I shall give him shall never thirst; but the water that I shall give him shall be in him a well of water springing up into everlasting life.
14) The woman saith unto him, Sir, give me this water, that I thirst not, neither come hither to draw
15) Jesus said unto her go call thy husband and come hither.
16) The woman answered and said I have no husband:
17) Jesus said to her you have well said you have no husband, for thou has had five husbands, and he whom thou now have is not thy husband; in that saidst thou truly.
18) The woman saith unto him, sir, I perceive that thou art a prophet. Our fathers worshipped in this mountain, and ye say, that in Jerusalem is the place where men ought to worship.

19) Jesus saith unto her, Woman believe me, the hour cometh when ye shall neither in this mountain, nor yet at Jerusalem worship the father.
21) Ye worship ye know not what.
22) We know what we worship for salvation is of the Jews.
23) But the hour cometh and now is when the true worshippers shall worship the father in spirit and in truth; for the father seeketh such to worship him.
24) God is a spirit and they that worship him must worship him in spirit and in truth.
25) The woman said unto him, I know that the Messiah cometh, which is called Christ when he come, he will tell us all things.
26) Jesus saith unto her, I that speak unto thee am he.
27) And upon this the disciples came, and marvelled that he talked with the woman; yet no man said what seekest thou? Why talkest thou with her?
28) The woman then left her waterpot, and went her way into the city, and saith to the men...
29) Come see a man which told me all things that ever I did, is not this the Christ?

***

Samantha is my name. For centuries, theologians, scholars, preachers and teachers have attempted to tell my story, but no one can tell it like me. I come from a family in which infidelity was common place. In other words, both of my parents cheated on each other. As a child, I saw this behavior when I was supposed to be out of sight and fast asleep if you know what I mean. There was always something going on at my house. When my parents were not arguing and fighting, they were busy helping out the church with their programs or busy at work. During my upbringing, I didn't spend a lot of time with my mother and father. Everytime I would ask my parents if we could do things together they were too busy and had excuses for their schedule with work and our church work.

Consequently, I spent a lot of time with my uncle and aunt. My uncle always played with me and helped me put my cartoon puzzles together.

Sometimes he would make silly faces to make me laugh, but he would also make me cry when he would ask to see my navel. When I raised up my dress, he would fondle me. I hated when he would do that. I remembered how scared I was of him as a young child. My uncle was 6'5" and 350lbs. I decided never to tell my parents, because I thought he would physically hurt me and my parents. There was already enough violence in my home with my parents arguing every weekend. I would hear my mother pleading and crying for my father to stop hitting her. I tried to drown out my mother's cries by reading out loud to myself. I was closer to my mother than my father. My father was a strict man, not much for words.

The more I tried to get my parents to spend time with me, the more irritated they became with me. They would remind me of all the things that they had bought me and would tell me that I should be grateful with what I have and understand their schedules. I didn't know then how to tell them that a simple hug would have been much better than all the dolls, clothes, and toys they bought me. I recall as a young girl promising myself that once I got older and ready to marry, I would be a faithful wife and spend lots of time with my children.

Please understand, I didn't share my experiences about my upbringing to justify the actions and choices I made in my adulthoood. I wanted to expose the affect of the inherited behavior and attributes that followed me.

Little did I know, everything I was exposed to as a child: deception, infidelity, violence, and violation was a tool that would shape my vulnerabilities, perceptions, and choices later in life.

As you have read in the beginnng of this chapter, I had five divorces and one convenient relationship. My reputation with men preceeded me, and I was known throughout the land to some as a "woman of the night," a "street walker", or in your modern day vernacular, a flat out "ho." The truth was, I had many deep voids in my life. I had needs to fulfill and an uncontrollable, unquenchable thirst for love. Allow me to give you a brief insight into each one and why they dissolved.

FIRST HUSBAND - KEVIN

All of my girlfriends were getting married and moving away from home. They met their Knights in shining armor at the famous well. I often looked for a man at the well, but none ever came through when I went to fetch water. I thought to myself, perhaps I should come earlier than they did each morning. I wasn't choosy, I would have married a crippled old man to just get away from my dysfunctional parents. I was so tired of going to weddings and coming home by myself. Every night, I dreamed of my wedding day. Then one day, while going to the well very early to fetch water, I met a man named Kevin. He was a tall, handsome and muscular man. He broke public customs and greeted me and told me how beautiful my red hair was. That was a big deal to me! You see, the custom of our culture held that men could not speak to women in public or vice versa, especially if they were not married. I thought to myself, perhaps this is my husband from God. At least three mornings out of the week I would run into Kevin. I started looking forward to seeing him and hoping each time that he would come by the well. I tried on his last name to see if it fit along with my first name and it was perfect. "Samantha Epstein."

After months of meeting him, and sneaking away by the trees to play with each other, we finally failed the abstinence test. I didn't want it to be like this, but I didn't know how much longer I could wait, nor did Kevin. His occupation as a merchant required that he make frequent trips out of town delivering goods from country to country. He told me that he dreamed of me night and day when he travelled on long journeys. The guilt and shame of our act haunted me every day. I hoped we would get married soon since we had been intimate. Kevin tried to tell me that it wasn't so bad, because we loved each other. I still felt horrible. I had my dreams of how my first sexual experience would be, and it wasn't under a shade tree on the side of a mountain. I started hinting to Kevin about marriage, and he would always change the subject. Each time he came to town, he wanted to have sex. How come he hadn't talked about marriage? I proved to him that I loved him by giving him sex. What else was supposed to happen? I began to feel used, but I was determined to hang in there because I believed that he would marry me.

I talked with my friend Janese about Kevin. She made me mad when she said to me, "why should he marry you, when you're giving it to him free." She didn't understand that he did love me, and that we were only trying to get to know each other better before we tied the knot. Plus, I wanted to be married so bad, and I wasn't about to let her discourage me. One year later, Kevin shocked me by giving me an engagement ring and asking my hand in marriage. I screamed "Yes!" We were married at Sychar Temple the next week. I was so happy.

Initially, his travelling job was not a problem for us because we found that the distance kept the newness in our marriage. It also made sex that much more fulfilling. Later, his job assignments became longer, ranging from two to three months. I didn't like this change, and I asked him if there was something that he could do. He told me that he had to accept whatever assignments his scheduling officer gave him.

One day while I was preparing to wash his uniforms, I discovered an envelope in his pocket containing a picture of a woman with two young boys. The inscription on the back read "To my dearest Kevin, we love you. Love, Sharon, Joseph & Mica", and had a recent date. I was devastated. I couldn't believe what I was reading. Could this be true? I asked myself. He never talked about being married before. Then I thought of so many other things I chose to ignore in the past that started to make sense to me. Kevin was almost finished with a two month assignment and was scheduled to be home in two weeks, which seemed to be the longest two weeks ever.

The moment he walked in the door, I confronted him about the picture. He was speechless. Then he told me that they had gotten a divorce years ago. When I asked why I was never told of his previous marriage, he replied "You didn't ask." I asked how did he get the current picture, and he calmly told me that she mailed it to his job at the children's request. I wanted so badly to believe him, so I did. After two weeks of him being home, he received another two month assignment. At first, I felt confident about him going because we had an incredible two weeks together. Kevin reaffirmed his love for me and our future together. Looking for him everyday after his two month assignment became scary. He was not home when he said he would be. The two months turned into four months, which turned into six months. I waited and I waited, but he never came back.

It took me almost three years to stop telling myself, my family and close friends at temple that Kevin was on an extended assignment. I drank for those three years while telling myself that he was coming back. I eventually had to file the necessary divorce papers for a marriage that was not valid because, he was already married.

SECOND HUSBAND - JOHN

My second husband's name was John. We also met at the well. One morning while walking away with my pot, a young man to my left was walking fast toward me. He noticed that my pot was a bit heavy by the wavering of my walk. He politely offered to help me. I whispered, "Thank you," to make sure no one heard me. John was a nice soft spoken man. He had such a boyish way about himself and told me that he loved to laugh and have fun. We talked while we walked. I learned that he was a widower of three years. His wife died from cancer two years after their marriage. He said I reminded him of her by the way I talked. I extended my condolences and wished him well. He switched the conversation by asking me about myself. I kept my answers brief, too ashamed to talk about my failed marriage. I gave him a brief synopsis of my first marriage and said I really didn't want to talk too much about my past. He respected my wishes.

When we arrived at the doorstep of my home, I thanked him and wished him a good day. It was obvious he did not want our conversation to end, so he quickly asked if I had room in my life for another friend. I relunctantly said yes, hoping I wasn't making another bad mistake to let this man into my life.

Surprisingly, I found spending time with John very uplifting. John was forever making me laugh with his cute jokes. Since the first day I met John, I never had to lift another water pot. He was there faithfully every morning to do it for me and to walk it to my doorstep. When we were not laughing and joking, we nurtured each others' wounds from our painful relationships and their abrupt endings. After a year of courting, we figured we were made for each other.

In the beginning of our marriage everything seemed to continue to go smoothly. Then after just eight months, John began reminiscing about his previous wife, Ellen. This behavior got so out of control, he started comparing me to Ellen. When I folded his clothes, he criticized the way I handled his T-shirts. He would unfold them demonstrating that he was used to them being folded a certain way and wished I did them that way as well. I bit my lip and decided that I could do that. Then his longing and depression over his previous wife caused him to sleep in our guest room not wanting to be close to me. This went on for weeks at a time. I still tried to be affectionate and kind, but he would reject any kind of holding and kissing, and he would tell me not to touch him. I crumbled inside from the rejection of my own husband.

One day while passing in the hallway, he told me that he should not have married me. I was dumbfounded at his words. "What do you mean you should have never married me?" I asked. He told me that he did not love me like I loved him, and that he was only filling a void in his life that Ellen still occupied. I was hurt. I had to go get a drink. As I drank, I told myself that I had to fight for my marriage and that he was only going through a phase. So, I decided to pray him through his mourning season. The more I left him to himself, the more comfortable he became with the distance between us. I felt like I was now living with a roommate who exchanged niceties every morning instead of a husband. During my many nights of sleeping alone, I couldn't help but reflect on him saying that he should not have married me and that he was only filling a void. He didn't love me. How could that be? I thought. I found myself regretting our union. As the old saying goes, hindsight is always 20/20. Obviously, he wasn't as healed and resolved with the death of his previous wife as he thought. Maybe he was in denial for the three years he thought he mourned over her death. Then I thought about my previous relationship. Maybe I wasn't over my pain of my first marriage as well. Then the scary question came to mind. Did we truly love each other? Of course, I loved him. I thought to myself. Or was I too filling a void.

After many months of living his life in seclusion, he told me that he could not handle being married to me or any woman for that matter. He discovered that his heart was in the grave with Ellen. He confessed again that he was trying to create another Ellen in me which would fill the void of her absence. Consequently, he didn't love me at all. He just liked all the things about me that reminded him of Ellen. We divorced.

THIRD HUSBAND - ROBERT

I met my third husband by the well one morning. Robert was wealthy after inheriting a sizeable fortune from his father. After courting Robert for two months, we decided to get married. Robert bought us a beautiful home on the hills of Samaria. I could look over the many pastures below. It was breathtaking. Robert was very outgoing and enjoyed inviting guests over to socialize. I really believed he just loved flaunting his wealth. Robert was the first hsuband who wanted to start a family with me.

After months of trying and planning, it finally happened, I was pregnant. Everyone in the town was happy. The women from the temple were very excited. They were planning baby showers in my second month of pregnancy. I must say it was a beautiful feeling to finally be a mommy and wife. It looked as if my dreams were finally coming true.

One day I came home early from visiting my parents, and walked into the house. As I entered our bedroom, I heard the most uncomfortable noises. I stood in the doorway with my mouth open. I was frozen, I couldn't breathe. There before me was my husband in bed with his best friend Derek, who was also the best man at our wedding. I continued to stand their long enough for his friend to get dressed and leave the house. Robert defended himself by telling me it was my fault. He said I didn't know how to make him feel like a man anymore. I quickly apologized and begged Robert to please give me another chance to be a good wife and a mother. He said he would give me thirty days. After three weeks he left me, and said I "wasn't wife material." Then he said the house would be up for sale, and that I was to be out in two weeks. He was gone. Another husband gone, just like that. I immediately started cleaning up the house, washing clothes, and singing to myself. I had to keep busy and distract myself from the reality of what had happened. I didn't want to feel any pain or anything, so I didn't think about it anymore. I tried to be the best wife a man could ever have in those three weeks, but it just wasn't good enough. Later on that same night, I sat up and drank myself into a drunken stupor. Then I started scratching myself and hitting myself. I thought about the baby I was carrying, and decided I had to find a way to kill it. I wasn't about to be a single mother bearing a child by a bi-sexual man. I stuck a sharp object in my inside, trying to kill the baby and almost killing myself. It was painful, but my humilation and anger toward Robert numbed me while I stabbed myself over and over. Each time I inflicted bodily pain, I could hear "You are not wife material." My emotions took over completely. After having to be rushed to a medical facility, I told the physicians that I was having a miscarriage. Two months later, Robert gave me a bill of divorce and a large settlement dowry. I guess he felt guilty for cheating on me.

FOURTH HUSBAND - LLOYD

After five years, my girlfriend Janese talked me into going on my first blind date. She assured me that he was unlike any man I had ever known or met. She was trying to get me out of the house to have some fun for a change. I must admit, I was afraid of being hurt again. She assured me that she and her husband would double date with us if I decided I wanted to go. I told her fine, set it up but, they better be there. I admit, I was lonely, I was depressed, I was even tired of masturbating. It had been five long years since I let a man lay his eyes on me, let alone his hands. They say that time heals all wounds, and throughout those five years of a recluse, surely time should have healed whatever was in me.

I took Janese up on her offer to double date. Lloyd was very nice and such a gentleman. When I learned that he was a doctor, I was impressed. He was a learned man. The first evening was nice, formal and kind of exciting. I was happy that I accepted the invitation. Lloyd and I started going out alone after a month of double dating. After a couple of dates, I began to feel awkward because he was not trying to have sex with me yet. I couldn't help but feel that something was very wrong with me. Maybe I wasn't attractive. Was he like my previous husband? God, I hoped not! He finally told me how much he respected me as a woman that believes in God, and I was a faithful attendee at my local Synogague. He didn't know that I was going there with my parents since childhood. That didn't necessarily say anything about my personal committment, but more about my personal habit. I thanked him for the compliment, but remained skeptical. Could a man respect a woman that much, to not try to provoke her sexually?

Lloyd eventually got around to asking me if I had ever thought about marrying a good man. I laughed! He laughed with me. He told me that he knew about my past and the unfortunate expriences that I had gone through.

I didn't know that Janese filled him in on everything about me. I didn't tell her she could do that.

From that evening on, I tried brushing him off because I was unable to accept that he knew about my past and still wanted me in his life. It would never work. He had never been married, and I didn't think I was the right type of woman for him as his first wife. He was so nice. I felt he deserved better. The more I tried brushing him off, the closer he kept coming with love, patience, and compassion. One day he walked up to me and kissed me without warning. He held me in his arms and gently said, "Stop trying to push my love away, I'm not going anywhere. I will wait for you until you're ready for my love. It's you that I want, I don't care about where you come from, Samantha." I didn't know how to handle his words. I shared with him that I wasn't used to being treated with so much consistent love. Lloyd convinced me to stop running from him and to give him and our relationship a chance. I finally agreed, and we were married within a month. I thought we were moving a bit fast, but Lloyd said it didn't take forever to know what he wanted. I was so caught between the fear of having him, but more petrified of loosing him.

Several months after our marriage, I found myself inciting arguments and making accusations about his whereabouts when he was not home at a certain time. I also found myself getting jealous when he wasn't home from work on time. I didn't want to respond like this, but I couldn't control my emotions. Lloyd would tell me over and over, that I could trust him in a room with a thousand women. That was not the best example he could have used, because that made it harder for me to believe him. I knew he was only trying to convince me that he was faithful to our relationship. I just could not stop thinking about all the other outcomes of my previous marriages, and asking myself why should this one be any different.

Lloyd was truly the best man I had ever met. He was consistent in everything he did and said. Furthermore, he didn't come with a lot of baggage that I and my other husbands came with. He didn't have another wife with children, like my first husband. His heart wasn't still in the grave with a deceased wife like my second husband, and he wasn't bi-sexual like my third husband. He was secure and content within himself. He had a confidence that was assuring, yet not overbearing. He had a love for God that caused him to treat me like a respectable wife. But in spite of all the points and glory around this man, my fears, jealousy, and inability to trust, hardened my heart from being open to him. The very love I dreamed of having was standing right in my face frustrating me with his unconditional love.

Lloyd knew about my inner struggles. My emotional state, was a mess. Again, I started hanging out at places where they drank. One night I ended up going home with a total stranger. I woke up the next morning in his bed totally surprised. Sadly enough, that was not the first or last time it happened.

After Lloyd found out about the extra marital affairs, he wanted us to go to counselling. I didn't want to. I just wanted our fairytale marriage to be over. I hurt this man so badly, I could not stand to keep sending him through my madness. I knew he didn't deserve to be treated like that. More than that, I knew he didn't deserve a woman like me. I had destroyed our marriage with all the baggage that I repeatedly denied was there and was not prepared or willing to deal with. I filed for divorce because I knew that he would never divorce me. I gave him the papers after the divorce was completed. I will never forget the last words he spoke to me. He told me that he would always love me and pray for the day that I could one day be free from the bondage of my past.

FIFTH HUSBAND - MICHAEL

I made up my mind that I would go to worship service, mind my own business, and go home. One day while leaving the synogogue, a man approached me. He was very handsome. He looked me right in my eyes and told me that God came to him and told him that I was his wife. That was a new line if I ever heard one. I didn't even think to question him. Could a man lie on God? I thought to myself. Michael was one of the assistants to the spiritual leader in our synogogue. The community held him in such high esteem.

After eight months of dating, Michael said we should be married before we were tempted to dissapoint God with our fleshly thoughts and emotions. I wasn't really having a problem, but I knew Michael was. We got married. I can't say that I was in love with Michael, but he said he loved me, and plus he said God told him I was his wife.

Not long after the "I do's" were said, I discovered that Michael had a quick temper, which he conveniently hid while we were courting. He didn't display any kind of temper problems when we were courting, but he sure did right after we were married. I shall never forget our first argument. I didn't make a big deal out of it because he didn't hit me. He just backed me up in a corner and started yelling at me. I must admit, he did scare me. I would witness this kind of behavior at least once a week over the course of the next three months. It usually happened when Michael came home from the temple after having a bad day. How do you have a bad day at God's house? I wondered to myself.

One day we were discussing something very trivial, and I didn't agree with his opinion. I didn't think I was being disrespectful, I just simply didn't agree. Before I could look up, he had slappped me. Within seconds, he quickly apologized, and said he had never done that before. I was shocked not knowing what to do or say. I kept quiet that whole afternoon. After that day, for two weeks, he brought me beautiful roses and attentively made love to me, trying to prove how sorry he was.

I couldn't talk with anybody at the synogogue because of his position there, and I didn't want to make him look bad over one mistake. I refused to talk with my parents who didn't seem to like him anyway, so I just prayed about it and hoped it would never happen again. Two months later he hit me again after a holy feast that we attended. A gentlemen walked up to me to give me a kind compliment about my dress. Michael accused the man of flirting. I laughed and told Michael he wasn't flirting. Michael took me by the hand and rushed me outside. He started hollering at me accusing the man who was making small talk with me. Then he said, he was tired of me not agreeing with him. I tried to tell him that the man was not making a pass at me. Then, I recognized that he was getting angrier and angrier and I tried to calm him down, explaining the story again. It was too late. He quickly grabbed me by the neck choking me and thrusting me to the ground. No one could hear us over the loud festivities that were happening on the inside.

I sat on the porch before going back in. Michael came back and told me that it was my fault that he grabbed me. He said if I didn't talk back to him and provoke him, it wouldn't have happened. I apologized for interrupting him and provoking him, accepting it was my fault.

After that night, I knew I was in trouble, but didn't know how to get out. I felt trapped and confused. I was hoping he would stop, but Michael's unpredictable acts of rage worsened.

The next month I had a surprise for Michael. I thought it may create another level of love in our house. I was pregnant. I coud not wait to tell Michael. As soon as he walked in from work, I had dinner ready as always and his bath drawn just the way he liked it to be. After dinner, I told him the surprise news about us having a baby. At first I was sure he said "Oh no." He asked me if I thought this was a good time. I didn't know quite how to answer his question. I didn't expect to have to go through an interrogation about being pregnant by my husband. Before he knew it, he asked how did it happened? I was still dumbfounded. He corrected himself by saying "I thought you were carefully counting days." I told Michael that I thought he would be jumping for joy, because we never talked about it one way or the other. He told me I should have thought about his schedule and the demand on his life at the synagogue. I screwed up again, I thought to myself. I personally thought it was refreshing news, but not to Michael. What man would not be excited about becoming a father? I was not about to get rid of this baby, like I did my other one. I was still being haunted by that foolish act, and I decided never to do it again. I will never forgive myself for killing my first baby. After that conversation about me being pregnant, I never brought the subject up again and neither did Michael. I didn't even tell anybody at the temple for fear of them mentioning it to Michael. What man can't rejoice about a child of his coming into the world? I didn't understand it, but I certainly didn't hassle him about it.

The days and weeks continued to go by. I spent most of my time just trying to keep peace in my home and not upset Michael. Michael was a totally different man at the synagogue than he was at home. I knew I was in trouble, but I just didn't know how to deal with it. I wished so many times to have someone to talk with that could teach me how to deal with this kind of problem. During the course of more intimidating encounters with Michael, I told myself to just leave. Part of me did not feel justified, because he had not hit me again since I became pregnant. I felt fortunate that I was pregnant, because I was protected.

Eventually, the abuse resumed until I was admitted to the hospital with a broken rib cage and busted ear drum. He beat me so bad, I lost the baby. His outbursts escalated to him beating me to the ground and then kicking me in my head. I lived in a woman's shelter until our divorce was final and my fear to live alone was over. He continued his ministry at the synagogue.

I concluded that all Michael wanted was a license to "screw", have full control over me, and a venting bag to hit on every now and then to let out his frustrations. He did not want a family. I promised myself, I would never get married again in my life.

SIXTH MAN - ERRON

After five failed marriages, I decided to stop the madness. I decided I would live my life free of any commitments, vows and responsibilities. I was so bitter and broken, I didn't care what came into my life.

The next man that came into my life was just like me. We discovered that we both had been in countless, worthless relationships and neither of us was looking for anything called marriage or commitment. We frequently laughed and cried as we shared our war stories over drinks. We agreed to be friends and whatever else we needed to be for each other's convenience.

I discovered I was having my first "shack attack." In case you ladies don't know what that is, it is living with a man you're not married to. It's sleeping with a man that you have no vows with, no strings, no ties, no accountability, no responsibilities, no promises to be broken, and no commitments to hold on to. I had really become the talk of the town. I was the household name at dinner tables, a topic at religious meetings, and the joke at the well, when women would gather to fetch water.

I disassociated myself from the community, the synagogue, and finally, God. All those years in the synagogue, I was only going out of culture, custom, and habit. I really stopped going so frequently, because I felt the people were always judging me. I couldn't feel comfortable in God's house.

I rearranged everything in my life to avoid any embarrassment. I would only come out to fetch water later, when I knew the community women had already left. I wore a black veil to the well to protect myself from the scorching sun and to be incognito. This way, I was clear and free of any confrontations, judgements, or snickering.

I reflected on my life each afternoon while going to fetch water from that famous well. That is where all my heartaches started. All I wanted was love. Why could I not find simple love? Now I have stooped to shacking with a man that's not even mine.

BEHOLD, THE 7TH MAN

Just when I thought I was having another typical day on my way to the well, I met my SEVENTH MAN. In the distance, I saw a figure of a medium size man leaning against the well. As I approached him, he appeared to be weary in strength. He was a brown skinned, gentle looking man. His eyes were piercing when he looked at me. The sun beamed on His dark, thick, brown textured hair.

I found him to be unlike any man I'd ever met. Even now, I don't have the appropriate words to adequately describe what I felt in HIS presence. I must admit when I first saw him, I thought he was another potential husband for some woman to find at the lucky well. I didn't understand at first, but it became clear to me as our conversation unfolded. He spoke to me with a voice of authority and compassion. He was a man of definite purpose and was on a mission.

He spoke about his primary mission for coming into the world. He was here to openly demonstrate God's love for His people by saving them from their sins. Then He made His mission personal, as if it were only between He and I. He said He knew I'd be here today. He said he came to save my soul and to set me free.

Of course, on every Sabbath day we consistently heard teachings of the coming Messiah, but never did I know that I would meet Him face to face. The moment God's love opened my eyes to see his very Son standing in front of me, I knew He was the Messiah, the Savior of the World. God loved me so much that He sent his only begotten Son to my common place to meet me right where I was to change my life forever. He will meet you too, right where your common place may be. While in His presence, I realized nothing else mattered to me. No hurts, pains, disappointments, or needs were necessary during that time with Jesus. At times, I couldn't help but smile and giggle girlishly. Then there were moments of uncontrollable tears from the powerful presence and prophetic purpose that He spoke about for my life. He knew everything about me, yet He still loved me. He spoke bodaciously and unashamably about the love of God concerning me to the point that I had to ask him again, if he had the right woman, at the right well. "Do you really know who I am?" I asked.

> "Yes Samantha, you are Mine and you are forgiven for all of your sins. You were created in My image and likeness. You are beautiful in the eyes of God. I know about your childhood pain, and rejections. I also know about your adulthood choices and regrets that you secretly lived with, but I have come to you that you may have life and life more abundantly. I don't look upon you as a "has been," but I look at what you shall be in Me.

When He spoke my name it was like a sword piercing my heart. He knew me. I didn't even tell Him my name.

Although the time I spent with Jesus was not as long as I had wanted it to be, it felt like years. I was consumed by every word that He uttered. His words felt like they added life to my very being and years to my future. I wanted to hear more. I decided to follow Jesus from that day forward. Over the course of time, I learned through Him how to walk out of my past by understanding it, and then embracing the spiritual principals and precepts given by my Heavenly Father. Jesus did not hold my past in judgement, instead He restored hope in my heart for my very life. He gave me a clear understanding about the distorted concepts of love that I learned from my childhood. He taught me:

1) The acts of infidelity that both my parents secretly mirrored planted a seed of unstableness and distrust in me.
2) The lack of nurturing during my upbringing created the neediness in me.
3) My parents workaholic and religious schedule subconsciously shaped my self-worth and attributed to my low-self esteem.
4) My uncle's continual molestations "in the name of love", as he would say, presented a distortion of what love is in my subconscious.
5) My lack of faith in my biological father hindered my faith and trust in God the Father.
6) He explained how a husband and wife are to love each other; that they would give their lives for each other. He told me that one day I will have that type of love and a family that mirrors true love.

After exposing the generational transferences which led me to a life of destructive behavior, He gently taught me about the healing love of God, and how to apply Godly principles and boundaries to my life. As I stood by that well with my pot in my hand, His truth liberated my very soul! I had never heard teachings like this before. He was so right when He said:

> "Whosoever drinketh of this water shall thirst again, But whosoever drinketh of the water that I shall give him shall never thirst; but the water that I shall give him shall be in him a well of water springing up into everlasting life."

I actually felt as though my cup had begun to run over that very moment. After my time with Jesus, I knew for the first time in my life who I was. When I received the revelation, and my eyes were opened to the fact that I was special to God, then I became special to me.

After this life-changing encounter with Jesus, I dropped my pot and ran into the city begging people to come see a man who told me all the things I ever did. Dropping my pot was symbolic of me breaking my old habits and ways, and leaving the well with new ways. When you have truly been set free you have no more shame, and no more past troubled reputation to be concerned with. That day I didn't care about our cultural customs of women speaking in public or any of those traditional rules. I only cared about men and women becoming free like me. I wanted them to know that the Deliverer had come, the Messiah was here. Please know that I was not perfect and everything didn't happen over night. My new life was a major healing process which contributed to four major factors:

1)My faith: I finally had real faith in God through my Lord and Savior Jesus Christ.

2) Prayer: I began like never before to worship God in spirit and in truth as Jesus explained.

3) Counselor: I also opened my life up for inspection and accountability to a sister that I met at worship. She knew of my circle of friends and associations. Consequently, she had gone through similar experiences. It was through her testimony that I was able to talk out my issues and process the years of pain and confusion. God appointed her to my life. Everyone needs a sister-friend. If you are open, God also has someone appointed for you.

4. Apply: This meant I had to apply the teachings and new ways of God's Word by living them.

Additionally, in this process, I learned how to live at peace with me. How to love me. How not to be afraid of being alone. I began to love myself, and I learned not to judge myself negatively just because I didn't have a man in my life. Ladies, love yourself first before you think you have to have someone to love you.

I am eternally thankful to God for providing everything I needed to help me walk through the process of healing. Because of his principals, I was able to stop the vicious cycle of dysfunctional relationships. I most of all thank God for His only begotten Son, the Messiah, Jesus the Christ who forgave me of my sins, taught and showed me the Truth, and gave me a fresh new start.

* * *

Chapter 5
BEHOLD, THE 7 TH MAN
SELAH! PAUSE, THINK, AND LET'S LEARN

Samantha's story is a classic example of what happens to children that grow up without a balanced environment comprised of Love, Protection,and Nurturing. It has been historically proven that by the time children reach the age of five, their character and personality are set in motion. They learn from the joys they have experienced, the traumas they have been exposed to,and the love they didn't receive. Therefore, it is at these primary years that we as parents, teachers, and leaders must ensure safe environments and healthy images for our trusting children as they grow into adulthood. The damaging messages mirrored and taught to our children will unfortunately transfer into their adulthood as a subtle translation of shame.

When children are exposed to acts of infidelity, it creates a picture of instability, distrust, fear, and confusion. Even when marriages end in divorce, the child feels divorced by that parent and within their subconsciousness believes they are a part of the problem. This plants the seed of insecurity and starts abandonment issues in the child. It sends devastating messages that say, "I don't love you anymore," "I don't want to be around you anymore." Divorce and infidelity destroy a child's self confidence, self-worth, value, and self esteem.

Finally, where molestation has occurred in the name of love, children are subject then to a distorted perception of what love is. The distorted concept teaches that sex is love. When a child is manipulated and intimidated to show love by touching or giving sex, he or she will grow up identifying love with sexual expressions.

Consequently, Samantha's childhood experiences followed her into her adulthood and into every marriage relationship she vowed to. Likewise, if we have been wounded, abandoned, confused or violated, we too will carry the same distorted messages they taught and characteristics they shaped within us.

Samantha ended up living a life of shame and embarrassment from a long line of bad relationships. She was reduced to wearing a black veil in the heat of the day while going to the well to fetch water. Her disguise helped her in avoiding public ridicule, scrutiny, and judgement. Until one day she met the 7th man at the well. Samantha met Jesus the Christ, the Messiah. She met up with the true man and she allowed herself to be truthful with him. Once she realized that the Healer was standing there in front of her, she gave him all of her wounds, pains, shame and voids to fill. She took off her black veil, dropped her pot and rejoiced, bringing others to the Savior to be saved and healed.

Ladies, until we honestly look at ourselves and become truthful about our pain, we can not move toward healing the inner woman. How do we participate in our healing? First, we must understand that our healing was provided over 2,000 years ago when Jesus Christ came to the earth to die for our sins. His blood allowed us access to the throne of Grace to ask help in time of need and time of sorrow. Jesus has made the first step, and now it's your turn to make the next step in receiving what He offers freely.

When a person receives salvation, no one comes up to that person and says "Be thou saved." God's Word tells us that, YOU must believe in YOUR heart that God sent His Son Jesus Christ to die for YOUR sins, and YOU must believe in YOUR heart that God raised him from the dead and that he sits at the right hand of the father making intercessions for YOU. For with the mouth man confesses and with the heart he believes unto righteousness. (Romans 10:9&10) YOU must invite the Holy Spirit to come into your life and direct your life from now on. Notice, you must do what is necessary to receive what God has already made available for you. The old myth that says when we get saved, our life becomes perfect. Not true. All of the pains and dysfunctions just don't politely go away, they must be put away and cast away from us. In order to put something away, you must acknowledge that it's there. My sisters, we can't be afraid of exposing the pains of our past for fear of being judged or appearing weak. Mind you however, through your relationship with Christ, God will direct you with whom, when, and where to share. He will also let you know what things are to be exposed to Him only. There is a saying, "we are as sick as our secrets," but my sister in the ministry, Dr. Martha Simmons says the correct rendering should say "we are sicker than our secrets." Jesus said He didn't come for those that were well, but for those that needed a physician. He came for those that had been brokenhearted, abused, outcast, in bondage, weary, sick, and confused. It's time to stop crying and complaining about the horrible past we've had when we have a Savior who is well able to heal us from the pains of our past. Jesus has given gifts to the body of Christ by way of Christian counseling, intercessory prayer, group therapy, and support groups. The Bible says:

> "Confess your faults one to another, and pray for one another that ye may be healed. The effectual fervent prayer of the righteous man availeth much." James 5:16.

Through confession, we expose the weakness, the faults, the pain, the anger, the bitterness, the unforgiveness, and the tormenting spirits that we have carried for years with us secretly. There is a supernatural dynamic when we are able to confess it. Confession it exposes the enemy, and He then loses the power to hold that dark secret, or hidden wound over your head. God does not judge us and label us dirty, guilty, unworthy, and cause us to feel ashamed.

I encourage every broken woman to love yourself enough to get the healing and help made available to you through the blood of Jesus Christ and the gifts that He has given to the body for edification, healing, instructions, and admonition. I declare in your hearing today, Yes, you can be a totally healthy woman. You can have healthy relationships. Yes, you can truly trust and love again by the transforming power of Jesus Christ!

CHAPTER 5
BEHOLD THE 7 TH MAN
Q&A's For Discussion

1. What did Samantha want most from her parents?
   a) Love
   b) Attention
   c) Family time together
   d) All of the above
   e) Other:______________________

2. What type of environment was Samantha raised in?
   a) Nurturing
   b) Damaging
   c) Dysfunctional
   d) Positive
   e) Other:_____________________

3. What significant relational patterns did she learn from her parents?
   a) Faithfulness
   b) Unfaithfulness
   c) Abusive
   d) Loving
   e) Trustworthiness
   f. Other:______________________

4. In Samantha's thoughts, how did she perceive her significance to her parents?
   a) Secondary
   b) In the way
   c) Rejected
   d) Their pride and joy
   e) Other:_______________________

5. How did Samantha's uncle impact her life?
   a) Negative
   b) Caused distorted views
   c) Damaging
   d) Crippling
   e) Other:________________________

6. When her parents used church work and domestic work as an excuse for not being able to spend time with Samantha, how did that shape Samantha's perception of her own worth and value?

7. Do you witness parents today placing careers, ministries, and hobbies over spending quality time with their children? What is detrimental and dangerous about doing this?

Marriages:

1. Reflect on your relationships and marriage(s). Does Samantha's life evoke any similar memories or experiences? What are they?

2. What type of emotional baggage did Samantha bring into her relationships from childhood?
   a) Abandonment issues
   b)Trust issues
   c) Neediness and desperation
   d) Low-self esteem
   e) Distorted concepts and expectations of love
   f) Fear
   g) All of the above
   h) Other:______________________________

3. What type of emotional baggage did she attract in her mates?
a) Controlling
b) Manipulative
c) Deceptive
d) Unfaithfulness
e) Abusive
f) All of the above
g) Other:______________________________

4. Why was it important to Samantha to marry her first husband?
a) Image
b) Neediness
c) Love
d) Obligation
e) Other:______________________________

5. Did Samantha demonstrate healthy boundaries in any of her dating process?
a) Never
b) Sometimes
c) Only one
d)Other:________________________

6. Do you believe Samantha healed properly from her first divorce?
a) Yes
b) No
c) Partly
d) Other:_______________________

7. What drew Samantha to her second husband John?
a) Love
b) Loneliness
c) Obligation
d) God
e) Other:_______________________

8. What drove her apart from her second husband?
   a) Love
   b) Loneliness
   c) Infidelity
   d) Lack of love
   e) Intimidation
   f) Other:________________________

9. What was the major problem that John had with Samantha?
   a) He didn't love her
   b) He was still in love with his previous wife
   c) He wasn't ready for marriage
   d) All of the above
   e)Other:_______________________

10. Do you think Samantha really loved John?
   a) No
   b) Yes
   c) Maybe
   d) Other:______________________

11. In Samantha's third marriage to Robert, do you think Robert's bi-sexual affair was Samantha's fault?
   a) Partly
   b) No
   c) Yes
   d) Unsure
   e) Other:_____________________________

12. How did Lloyd propose to deal with Samantha's emotional issues?
   a.) Prayer
   b.) Counseling
   c.) Loving her through them
   d). Facing them
   d.) All of the above
   e.) Other:___________________________

13. What prevented Samantha from having a healthy marriage with Lloyd?
a) Fear of love
b) Inability to trust
c) Not being healed from previous marriages
d) Emotionally unstable
e) All of the above
f) Other:______________________________

14. What type of man was Lloyd?
a) Good man
b) God fearing
c) Loving
d) Faithful
e) Compassionate
f) All of the above
g) Other:______________________________

15. In Samantha's fifth marriage why do you feel she stayed with Michael over ten years?
a) Religious pressure
b) Fear & intimidation
c) Low-self-esteem
d) Lack of self respect and love for herself
e) Other:______________________________

16. Why did Samantha down play Kevin's "scaring her to death" by his hollering and backing her up into a corner?
a) Because she didn't feel it was major
b) Because he didn't hit her
c) Because she felt he was justified
d) None of the above
e) Other:______________________________

17. What were the vices she used to help cope with her depression and emotional pain with Michael?
a) Promiscuity
b) Alcohol
c) Denial
d) All of the above
e) Other:_______________________

18. Do you see any similarities of Samantha's life in any of your past or present relationships?

19. How do you believe that healing from brokenness, betrayal, sexual violation and physical abuse occurs?
a) Time heals all wounds
b) Counseling
c) Prayer
d) Forgiving Self, and Mate
e) Facing the pain of it
f) Name it and claim it
g)Other:_______________________

20. The advice that Samantha received from her friends concerning Michael's behavior was:
a) Unrealistic
b) Insensitive
c) Dangerous
d) Foolish
e) All of the above
d)Other:_______________________

21. Did Samantha heal from any of her relationships before meeting Jesus?
a) yes
b)no
c)partly

22. Do you think that a person can be totally healed of past and present traumas instantaneously?
a) Yes
b) No
c) Maybe

23. Do you believe that a person has to re-visit the place of pain in order to heal from it?
a) Yes
b) No
c) Maybe

24. What was Jesus purpose for visiting Samantha?
a) To give her salvation
b) To heal her from her pain
c) To teach her God's Word
d) To restore her life
e) To liberate her mind
f) To open her eyes from doubt and deception
g) All of the above
h) Other:______________________________

25. What did Samantha learn from Jesus?
a) Generational curses that transfers to each generation
b) The failure of being loved and nurtured causes neediness
c) The act of sexual violation presents distorted concepts of love
d) The lack of fatherly love and attention hinders healthy adult bonding
e)Without teaching spiritual/moral boundaries, life is destructive & emotionally damaging
f) Other:______________________________

26. What did he teach her about her self-worth?
a) She was created in his likeness and image
b) She was worth dying for
c) Other:______________________________

27. What did Jesus know about Samantha?
a) Everything
b) Her past
c) Her future
d) Her purpose
e) All of the above
f) Other:______________________________

28. At anytime during Jesus' conversation with Samantha, did he judge her?
a) No
b) Yes
d)Other:_____________________________

29. How would you describe Samantha's relationship with Jesus?
a) Powerful
b) Effective
c) Wonderful
d) Life saving
e) Life changing
f) All of the above
g) Other:____________________________

30. What did Jesus instill in Samantha's mind and heart?
a) Hope
b) Joy
c) Self-esteem
d) Love
e) Forgiveness
f) Other:________________________________

31. What was the process that contributed to Samantha's healing?
a) Prayer
b) Counseling
c) Faith
d) Application
e) Other:______________________________

32. Have you learned any valuable lessons and principles from the life and relationships of Samantha?

What does God offer to the soul that thirsteth In Isaiah 55:1-3?

____

____

According to II Corinthian 5:17 what happens to the individual who believes on Christ?

____

____

Chapter 6

RUN MARY RUN, HEROD WANTS TO KILL YOUR BABY

Luke 1:26-38(KJV)

26) And in the sixth month the angel Gabriel was sent from God unto a city of Galilee, named Nazareth,

27) To a virgin espoused to a man whose name was Joseph, of the house of David; and the virgin's name as Mary.

28) And the angel came in unto her, and said, Hail, thou art highly favored, the Lord is with thee; blessed art thou among women.

29) Troubled at his saying, and cast in her mind what manner of salutation this should be.

30) And the angel said unto her, fear not Mary for thou hast found favor with God.

31) And, behold thou Shalt conceive in thy womb, and bring forth a son, and shalt call his name Jesus.

32) He shall be great, and shall be called the Son of the highest; and the Lord God shall give unto him the throne of his father David.

33) And he shall reign over the house of Jacob for ever, and of his kingdom there shall be no end.

34) Then said Mary unto the angel, How shall this be, seeing I know not a man?

35) And the angel answered and said unto her. the holy ghost shall come upon thee, and the power of the highest shall overshadow thee; therefore also that holy thing which shall be born of thee shall be called the son of God.

36) And, behold thy cousin Elizabeth, she hath also conceived a son in her old age; and this is the sixth month with her, who was called barren.

37) For with God nothing shall be impossible.

38) And Mary said, behold the handmaid of the Lord be it unto me according to thy word. And the angel departed from her.

***

Wedding bells had been ringing in my ears all month long as the days were growing nearer. The date of my marriage to my only love. I would count the days, minutes and seconds to that very moment of saying, "I do". I often envisioned the entire ceremony. I would think on how life would be with Joseph. I found myself twirling around and around in my living room as if Joseph and I were on a ballroom floor. Gracefully dancing, I felt as if I were on a carousel as I laughed with anticipated joy. While twirling around the third time, suddenly, appearing in front of me was a radiant, tall, Angelic being. At first I was afraid because of the sudden appearance. I didn't know what to say or what to do. The Angel quickly calmed me with his peaceful words as he said,

> "Fear not, Mary, for thou has found favour with God. And, behold thou shalt conceive in thy womb, and bring forth a son, and shalt call His name Jesus. He shall be great, and shall be called the son of the highest; and the Lord God shall give unto Him the throne of His father David: and He shall reign over the house of Jacob for ever, and in His kingdom there shall be no end."

I asked him, how should this be, seeing that I had never been intimate with a man. With a gentle smile, he said:

> "The Holy Spirit will come upon you, and the power of the Most High will overshadow you; and for that reason the holy offspring shall be called the Son of God. And Behold, even your relative Elizabeth has also conceived a son in her old age; and she who was called barren is now in her sixth month. For nothing will be impossible with God.

I stood there reflecting on the many times my father sat the family down at each eating time whether it be breakfast, lunch, or dinner and communed with us about the coming Messiah. He spoke of the prophets and their prophesies about our deliverer, but not once did I ever envision him! I was overwhelmed. I was speechless, dumbfounded, and humbled at this great news. I only had enough strength to say,

"At thy word let it be done unto thine handmaid."

I hid my face in my hands crying my tears of joy and fear. Seconds after I looked up, the Angel was no longer there. Moments after his dissapearance, I could hear his words as if they were spiritually branded on the front of my heart and still echoing in my ears.

I jumped for joy dancing unto the Lord like David danced when he delivered the Ark of the covenant back to the children of Israel. I began to praise and worship God as if I were going out of my mind. Finally, once I sat down from my exhaustive experience, I saw Joseph's face. Then I saw my parents face. Then there was the entire community in my mind. Who would explain this miracle to them? How would they understand this whole assignment? What would they say? How could I explain what I believed in my heart? I asked myself several questions one after another. My heart beating with fear, I came up with no logical answers of how this all came about. I decided that I would deal with that war, when I crossed that battlefield. I chose to just ponder the news in my heart.

The following morning, Joseph stopped by to visit with me. My mother came rushing in my room saying that Joseph wanted to see me quickly. At first, I was nervous and took my time coming out. I finally walked into the living room where Joseph was waiting for me. He wore a soft smile on his face. Somehow, I instantly knew that he knew. It was all in the way he looked at me and the way his eyes glistened with excitement. As soon as we were out of hearing range of my family, Joseph told me about the exciting dream he had the night before where an angel came to him. He wanted to confirm everything that the Angel had spoken to him in his dream. It was remarkable. He recited the Angels' words to me verbatim. I screamed, "Yes, Joseph, yes, it's real! That's exactly what happened! Joseph held me in his arms, whispering that he would protect me and the promised savior that was to come through me. We could not deny it. We knew it was real. I was so comforted to know that Joseph understood and accepted God's plans.

The following morning, I was laying in my bed. It was right before the fullness of daybreak, still dawn. Suddenly, I was awakened by an illuminating light which overtook my room. There weren't any noises or sounds, just a pronounced presence. As I slowly looked around, pulling my hair from my eyes, I didn't see any lanterns lit, or any wood burning in the fireplace. There was such an overwhelming peace. Then I knew. This was it! That which was spoken of by the Angel. I laid there not moving, with tears welling up in my eyes. My lips began to worship my Jehovah God for this great day that had come. The light seemed to grow brighter and brighter, but now it felt as if it was consuming me in it's presence. This light wasn't the sun rising in the east, but it was the Son setting inside of me. The Son of God. I could feel this light penetrating my entire being. I could not keep my eyes open from the powerful illumination. As the light consumed me, the brightness of the room began to slowly fade. It was incredible, yet it lasted for only a moment. I was with child now, of the Holy Ghost, with the Holy One, called the Son of God. He would be all that we learned of the coming Messiah: The Savior that would take away the sin of the world. Not only was He the Son of God, but He would also be Christ, The Messiah, Savior Redeemer, Wonderful Counsellor, Faithful Witness, The Word of God, The Truth, The Light of the World, The Way, The Good Shepherd, Mediator, Deliverer, The Great High Priest, The Author and Perfecter of Our Faith, The Captain of our Salvation, Our Advocate, The Son of Man, God, The Holy One of God; Only Begotten Son; Mighty God; Ruler of the Kings of the Earth, the King of Israel, King of Kings, Blessed and Only Potentate, Price of Life, Prince of Peace, the Son of David The Root and offspring of David, the Bright and Morning Star, Immanuel, the Second Adam, the Lamb of God, The Lion of the Tribe of Judah, the Alpha and the Omega, the First and the Last, the Beginning and the End, the Beginning of the Creation of God, and The First-Born of all creation. My Son would be a Hero to His people, and a liberator of all humanity.

I shall never forget that day, it was one of the happiest days in my life. I shared the second mysterious visitation with Joseph the next morning. We rejoiced and worshipped God together. We shared a secret that nobody in the entire world knew. Only Joseph, myself, my cousin Elizabeth, her husband Zacharias, and the entire host of Heaven.

Two months later, we were married and life certainly took on another drastic change for us. I made sure I took good care of myself, probably over and above any pregnancy. Then it happened. Somehow it became known amongst our family members that I was with child before Joseph and I were married. Then it seeped out into our neighborhood. This caused whispers and talk in the community. I was now accused of trying to hide an illegitimate child behind an arranged marriage to Joseph. People were actually counting the months of our marriage with the child that I was due to have. This also brought great danger to me and my family. Jewish customs were strict concerning such implications of deceit. A girl could be stoned for such trickery and betrayal. Joseph was not about to let anything happen to me. He kept his word as he promised to protect me and the baby at all cost. While our marriage was fresh and new, it quickly grew weary and challenging. Particularly, because we were unable to experience intimacy until the child was born. Joseph and I both struggled with our desires for one another and had to be strong for each other. Unfortunately, in Joseph's weaknesses, he would sometimes make statements that he immediately regretted. He remembered that the child I carried was not just any child, but the Son of the living God.

There were nights when Joseph couldn't sleep. He would quietly go into the living room. One night, I overheard Joseph praying and crying out to God about his struggles with my pregnancy and his manhood. He told God he was sorry for envying the conception. He confessed that he had longed for me to be the mother of his children, but now it was ruined because of the called and chosen assignment on my life. He actually told God that he felt as if he was competing with Him. I couldn't believe how real he was being with God about his jealousies, insecurities, and anger. He even asked God why did he choose me to be the one to carry His Son Jesus and not another woman who could not have children which would have made it more of a miracle. I couldn't believe what Joseph was saying to God. He then started rattling off about how he felt like a mistress instead of a husband. I must say after each confession to God, he would end it by telling him how sorry he was that he was feeling all these emotions. He even admitted that he was aware of God's sovereignty, but just didn't know how to deal with it. He asked God to please help him and strengthen him. I was moved by my husbands' clear transparency with God, and yet his protective nature toward trying not to subject me to his human frailties.

Life was also emotionally challenging for me toward the end. I needed Joseph's support and reaffirmation of his love for me and his verbal support of the child I was carrying. I felt I couldn't be too demanding because in reality, it really wasn't Joseph's baby. I'm sure if it were his, things would have been different during those lonely moments of distance between us. There were times I felt guilty, as if I did betray him, even though I knew better. I wanted to say so many times, "It's not my fault that God chose me to be the mother of His Son. I didn't apply for the position, it was assigned to me. I didn't go to school to become it, I was promoted from within. I knew the child would be born by a virgin girl, but I never envied the virgin girl that would be chosen. I was satisfied with my life as it was and was ready to be married to the man that I loved, Joseph." I thought to myself, if he could only really understand that it was difficult for me too. Oh, if I could just get that across to Joseph, life could be better for us. Life did calm down once we left our city and I came closer to my delivery time. I anticipated with great anxiety His manifested purpose in the world. I knew how great He would be and, I knew how powerful He would be. I remembered one of the prophesies from the prophet Isaiah: It was so powerful, I made sure I remembered it: These would be the words of the Messiah who was to come:

> THE SPIRIT OF THE LORD IS UPON ME; BECAUSE THE LORD HATH ANOINTED ME TO PREACH GOOD TIDINGS UNTO THE MEEK; HE HATH SENT ME TO BIND UP THE BROKEN HEARTED, TO PROCLAIM LIBERTY TO THE CAPTIVES, AND THE OPENING OF THE PRISON TO THEM THAT ARE BOUND.
>
> TO PROCLAIM THE ACCEPTABLE YEAR OF THE LORD, AND THE DAY OF VENGEANCE OF OUR GOD: TO COMFORT ALL THAT MOURN.
>
> TO APPOINT UNTO THEM THAT MOURN IN ZION, TO GIVE UNTO THEM BEAUTY FOR ASHES, THE OIL OF JOY FOR MOURNING, THE GARMENT OF PRAISE FOR THE SPIRIT OF HEAVINESS; THAT THEY MIGHT BE CALLED TREES OF RIGHTEOUSNESS, THE PLANTING OF THE LORD, THAT HE MIGHT BE GLORIFIED.
>
> AND THEY SHALL BUILD THE OLD WASTE, THEY SHALL RAISE UP THE FORMER DESOLATIONS, AND THEY SHALL REPAIR THE WASTE CITIES, THE DESOLATIONS.

AND STRANGERS SHALL STAND AND FEED YOUR FLOCKS, AND THE SONS OF THE ALIEN SHALL BE YOUR PLOWMEN AND YOUR VINEDRESSERS.

BUT YE SHALL BE NAMED THE PRIESTS OF THE LORD: MEN SHALL CALL YOU THE MINISTERS OF OUR GOD: YE SHALL EAT THE RICHES OF THE GENTILES, AND IN THEIR GLORY SHALL YE BOAST YOURSELVES.

FOR YOUR SHAME YE SHALL HAVE DOUBLE; AND FOR CONFUSION THEY SHALL REJOICE IN THEIR PORTION; THEREFORE IN THEIR LAND THEY SHALL POSSESS THE DOUBLE; EVERLASTING JOY SHALL BE UNTO THEM.

FOR I THE LORD LOVE JUDGEMENT, I HATE ROBBERY FOR BURNT OFFERING; AND I WILL DIRECT THEIR WORK IN TRUTH, AND I WILL MAKE AN EVERLASTING COVENANT WITH THEM.

AND THEIR SEED SHALL BE KNOWN AMONG THE GENTILES, AND THEIR OFFSPRING AMONG THE PEOPLE: ALL THAT SEE THEM SHALL ACKNOWLEDGE THEM, THAT THEY ARE THE SEED WHICH THE LORD HATH BLESSED.
I WILL GREATLY REJOICE IN THE LORD, MY SOUL SHALL BE JOYFUL IN MY GOD; FOR HE HATH CLOTHED ME WITH THE GARMENTS OF SALVATION, HE HATH COVERED ME WITH THE ROBE OF RIGHTEOUSNESS, AS A BRIDEGROOM DECKETH HIMSELF WITH ORNAMENTS, AND AS A BRIDE ADORNETH HERSELF WITH HER JEWELS. FOR AS THE EARTH BRINGETH FORTH HER BUD, AND AS THE GARDEN CAUSETH THE THINGS THAT ARE SOWN IN IT TO SPRING FORTH; SO THE LORD GOD WILL CAUSE RIGHTEOUSNESS AND PRAISE TO SPRING FORTH BEFORE ALL THE NATIONS.

Each time I recited that prophecy to myself, if filled me with tears of joy to know that our Saviour was here. My rejoicing was daily, however, I soon learned that in order to really have a true testimony, you must first have an appointed trial.

The Angel delivered his assignment. However, I concentrated more on the blessings of it, versus the burdens that were sure to come. I forgot the prophetic painful realities, rejections, and the stony road that we all would have to trod by this blessing. I failed to remember that my child would have to be born in a manger next to horses and cows because there were no emergency rooms available or hotels with vacancies. I failed to remember that there would be an enemy waiting to assassinate Him, who was none other than KING HEROD. I failed to remember that he would have a contract out on His life from the announcement of his arrival into the world told by three wise men. It never crosssed my thoughts that we would have to run from city to city, place to place to hide even to the deepest parts of Africa amongst our people to protect our Son. We knew they would never find us there. And out of all my selective memory, the Angel didn't remind us that Jesus would upset the political and religious world power.

And finally as if that were not enough, it hurt me and almost destroyed me to see that He had to be taken from court to court and sentenced for a crime He didn't commit. He had to die for a people that He loved and to bear a cross he couldn't carry. I didn't realize that I had to suffer the pain of watching my son die. Yes, I had to stand at the bottom of a cross watching my Son being nailed through His flesh and bones as His limp body lay on that rugged cross. There were only a few familiar faces there. Sometimes loved ones will disappear at the most obscure times in life, leaving you alone to do what God has called you to do. I didn't know that Joseph would not be with me until the bitter end. I was comforted though, because as my Son was giving His life for the world, he stopped dying to give me another son, John to care after me. I gave Him life during birthing Him into this world, but He gave me life while leaving this world for three awesome days to rise up and declare our salvation and great Victory in HIM! Not in me, but in Jesus! The calling on my life was one of great honor and humility. It required the Almighty God to bring it to pass and to sustain me and my entire family through it. I have learned many things, one of the most significant lessons of my life is that not everyone is happy when there is a calling on their life. Be it your pastor, your husband, your children, your teacher, your employer, your sisters girlfriends, and even yourself. Oh, at first they may smile, embrace, and congratulate you, but your calling will not necessarily win you a popularlity contest. In fact, smiles can sometimes turn into an upside down cold sneer. Your anointing may never be received by those around you. However, the number one priceless lesson will have to be the revelation and illumination of the Sovereignty of God. I have discovered it's His business who He chooses to use. I have learned that God has always come through for me. All I had to do was hold up and He continued to show up for every situation I faced. I can't doubt the goodness of the Lord and the power of his might. I thank Him for counting me a part of His salvation plan and honoring and granting me highly favored among women.

Chapter 6
RUN MARY, RUN, HEROD WANTS TO KILL YOUR BABY
SELAH, PAUSE AND LET'S LEARN

Mary was a chosen girl, and just like Mary, God has tapped on the doors of your spirit and has placed in you an irresistible calling that you cannot deny. That thing you cannot seem to forget. That thing within that arises at the most untimely moment. That which causes you to have sleepless nights. That thing that defies religious traditions and violates legal customs. Then I could be the very thing that longs to be born in the birth canal of your spirit that you have tried to block out with your constant business. Jeremiah 20:9 describes the callings of God like "fire shut up in your bones." Yes, that which he has placed in you, that holy calling, that will set people free, open blinded eyes, and heal broken hearts. That which will direct lost men, women, boys and girls directly to the Savior is in your heart. All that is required of you is to say like Mary, "At thy Word, let it be done unto thine handmaiden." You may have told God countless times that you do not qualify and are not the woman or girl for the job. Romans 8:29-31 tells us that

> "For whom he foreknew, he also predestined to become conformed to the image of his Son, that he might be the firstborn among many brethren; and whom he predestined these he also called; and whom he called these he also justified and whom he justified, these he also glorified. What then shall we say to these things? If God is for us, who is against us?"

All we need is the willingness to do His will. You must be willing to take the risk of rejection and being misunderstood. You must be willing to be called rebellious and out of line. Those that love you the most will shun you and those that you look to for examples and mentors may renounce you. But do not let them stop you! In Matthew 10:37 Jesus says "if you love mother or father more than me, you are not worthy of me; if you put anything before me, you are not worthy of me. Jesus had to face tremendous opposition and danger while coming into the world to save your soul and mine. Why? The scripture tells us in John 3:19-21 Jesus tells us:

> And this is the judgement, that the light is come into the world, and men loved darkness rather than the light; for their deeds were evil. For everyone who does evil hates the light, and does not come to the light, lest his deeds should be exposed, but he who practices the truth comes to the light, that his deeds may be manifested as having been done in God."

I am talking about divine purpose and destiny. You see, God has placed purpose in the life of every individual He has created, but everyone will not yield to the call, the gift, and the talent given for the Glory of God, because of their own desires and their own plans. Jeremiah 29:10 declares

> "I know the plans/thoughts I have toward you; and they are peace; and not evil; to give you a future and a hope and an expected end."

God is calling every born again woman, from the homemaker, school teacher, police woman, bus driver, cafeteria assistant, nurse, doctor, lawyer, secretary, musician, entertainer, judge, comedian, artist, writer, orator, director, producer, newscaster, agent, and on and on to spread his word (i.e. from teaching, preaching, evangelizing, singing, missionary, bereavement/elderly care, etc.) . Where? Everywhere. From the Sunday School Department to the School Board. From the Prisons to the Pulpit. From the back alley streets of Skid Row to the Halls of Congress. From the Chapels to Convalescent Homes. Near and far He is calling His daughters to spread the Word of salvation and redemption. I encourage you today to not let Satan stop the anointed seed that God has ordained for you. It does not matter where you have been, what you have been through, or what has been done to you, you qualify. Maybe you started in ministry and stopped because of mistakes you've made; God is bigger than your mistakes. God wants to restore you so that you can walk in your complete purpose. The Bible says the gifts and callings of God are without repentance which means God didn't change his mind. Romans 11:29 God is not wishy washy, like humans. The Bible says the righteous man falls, but he gets back up. So get up, wherever you are, and be like Moses who said "unless your presence is with me, I will not go, but with your presence with me, I will go." Satan knows that God has planted a seed of the divine purpose in your life as he did in Mary, but He wants you to believe you are not with Child of the Holy Ghost. Satan will tell you that the baby has died in your womb, but you must know that God is able to complete that which He has begun birthing in you. He will bring it to pass. The true reality is that it is finished in you all that God has made in you and called you to be. We just have to say like Mary, "be it done unto thine handmaiden." Satan will try to tell you to abort the spiritual child, you can't afford it right now. You have to believe that where God gives the vision, He also supplies the provision. You must wait on God. Satan will tell you to put your baby up for adoption for someone else more qualified, but you can't give to someone else what God has given to you. Satan will tell you that you are barren and nothing good can come out of you. You must remember that you were created in the image of God and in his likeness. You are fruitful! When the Devil comes to try and talk to you, run from those statements and run to the shelter of God who is your refuge and strength. Run into His pavilion of peace. Run daughters. Don't let the spirit of Herod kill your baby! Run beside the still waters and green pastures of God. Don't let the spirit of Herod kill your baby; run into God's arms that are able to keep you; run under God's banner that is able to protect you; don't let Herod kill your baby. God says, "you are going to have a healthy baby, don't worry. I'm in the delivery room with you, and I will tell you when to push, when to press, when to bear down, and when to rest. I'll be right there before, during, and after the delivery of your baby, and you will produce much fruit for the Kingdom." Now are you ready?

Chapter 6
RUN MARY, RUN, HEROD WANTS TO KILL YOUR BABY
Q&A's

1. According to Jeremiah 29:11, What does God give to his children?
a) Good thoughts
b) Hope and expectancy
c) Great plans
d) Promises
e) Other:______________________

2. According to Ephesians 4:8 Who gives us our gifts or callings on your life?
a) The Deacon Board
b) The Ministerial Staff
c) School
d) Parents
e) Our Lord and Savior
f) Other:______________________

3. Is there a cost for these spiritual gifts?
Yes or No?

4. According to Romans 11:29, what do you have to do to maintain your gift?
a) You have to keep qualifying to do the job
b) You must be academically astute
c) You must come from a great family
d) You must always do right in order to keep gift.
e) Other:______________________

5. According to Jeremiah 1:5 when did God ordain Jeremiah a prophet unto the nations?
a) After he finished going to school
b) After he got his life together
c) When Jeremiah became perfect
d) After Jeremiah finished sewing his wild oats
e) After he visited all of the sick in the community
f) Before he was even born in his momma's womb
g) Other:______________________

6. Who was the child that Mary carried in her womb?
a) John the Baptist
b) Jesus Christ
c) Jeremiah
d) Isaiah
e) None of the above
f) Other:__________________________

7. How does God choose whom He decides to use?
a) Multiple choices
b) By Race
c) By Color
d) His soveriegn will
e) Other:__________________________

8. God's primary purpose for calling us into his ministry is to:
a) Bring Glory to his name
b) Give Salvation to lost men and women
c) To show his love toward all mankind
d) Other:___________________________

9. According to Jeremiah 29:11 God sees our future. Study this scripture and list what God promises?

____

____

10. Study IITim 1:9 and write what type of calling God has called believers into?

____

____

____

11. According to Hebrews 3:1 we are apart of a ________________________calling.

CHAPTER 7
BEAUTY IN THE EYES OF GOD

A PROPHETIC EXHORTATION

Isaiah 61:3

Daughters of the Most High King, there is beauty in creation alone. God says to you, "When I made you, I made a good thing. Make no mistake about it! Don't forget it! When I developed you, I had a divine and distinct plan in mind on just how I wanted you to look. If humanity is not pleased with your outcome, be clear, that I am WELL pleased with you, because you're mine, and you are not the worlds. In my image and likeness I made you. I approved of you when I first envisioned you. I loved you upon shaping and forming you. I smiled at your presence as I ushered you delicately into your mother's womb. Then I made you with purpose. You are a lifegiver. Humanity can only come from your loins."

Daughters, be not pre-occupied with the scrutiny and vanity of this world. Rather, pursue and embrace the beauty of holiness, righteousness, humility, and grace. You need to understand that there is beauty in your creation alone. Before there was Maybelline, Revlon, Fashion Fair, Mary Kay, and Avon, there was beauty. Before there was lipstick, and lip gloss, there was beauty. Before there were eye shadows, blush, and foundations, there was beauty.

Before there were any cosmetics and beauty enhancers, there you stood alone in My beauty and in My expressed image. I looked at you and declared that you were GOOD before anyone else had an opinion, or a comparison. There were never to be two of a kind. I only made one masterpiece as you. No one else possesses what I have placed in you and around you. Your legs were not meant to look like everyone elses, so stop comparing yourself. Your eyes were not meant to be shaped like anyone elses, so stop condemning yourself. Your cheekbones and your lips were never intended to mirror others, so stop changing what I have made. Your buttocks, hips, and stomach were uniquely designed just for you, so stop hating yourself. Rather, be content in your special uniqueness and the fact that there is only one of you. You shall not only give an account of your financial stewardship of what I have blessed you with, but also of your life and body. Yes, you will give an account on how you loved MY daughter, which is you. Your stewardship extends and covers your entire personhood that I have given to you as a gift. My Word exhorts you to Love your neighbors as you love yourself. Which means, you must love yourself first before you can love your neighbor at all.

The old cliche' "What you see is what you get" does not fit the Woman I have made in you, because that which you see on your exterior does not touch the power and beauty graced in your spirit. Why? Because you are filled with the beauty of my Holy Spirit. You are never alone, but you have divinely appointed escorts (Father, Son & The Holy Ghost) where ever you go all the days of your life. You live in the best spiritual neigborhoods, for I have caused you to sit in heavenly places where you dwell in the secret place of the most high God. There is more to you than your beautiful smile, your outward appearance, and the depth of your knowledge and skills that you possess. You are my Queen that sits on a royal throne erected in heavenly places. When you speak, words of life follow, for out of your mouth comes wisdom and discretion. Fragrance of the sweetest myrrh fill your room and where you walk kingdoms come. You are wise and prudent in spending and lending. Your prudent ways reflect and represent my presence in your life. You work diligently and sweetly as unto me. Your ways are not presumptuous, but are divinely ordered by me. You are wise as a serpent, but you are also humble and meek as a dove soaring across her seas.

Your clothing is elegantly draped and flows with the winds upon your royal body adorning the masterpiece that I have made in you. The exploitation of your body will never come from you for you know it is sacred and secret and so you carefully guard it.

Your thoughts are thoughts of peace and not war. Your conversation brings out the best in all and edifies the downtrodden. You are beautiful and yet, you are so much more. Why? Because Daughter, there is more to you than meets the eye....

HOPE

by Jewel Turner

I was inspired today!
Inspired by the deep love and concern of a friend.
Inspired to open up the tightly shut windows of my soul.
Inspired to destroy the lock, padded by years of resentment,
pain, torture and passive death.

I was inspired today!
Inspired by compassion rooted in experience and watered by hope.
Inspired to step out of the darkness which surrounded and enveloped me.
Inspired to address the past but not live in it.

I was inspired today!
Inspired by the fear defying courage of a friend.
Inspired to lift up my head, bowed so long in shame.
Inspired to see the real beautiful me.

I was inspired today!
Inspired by and touched by a friend.
Inspired and touched by a friend.
Inspired and touched by a friend.

I was inspired today...
And while tomorrow will soon be called today,
a day of uncertainty;
I'm inspired by the fact that I look forward to it
through windows of hope, love and victory.

Jeremiah 29:11
"For I know the thoughts that I think
toward you, saith the Lord,
thoughts of peace, and not evil,
to give you an expected end.

Bibliography

Chapter 1

King James Version, *The Word in Life Study Bible* (Thomas Nelson Publishers, 1993), 1853,
473-483

(Book of St. John 4:1-29)

(Book of John 4:1-29) "whosoever drink of this water ....."

(Book of James 5:16)

Chapter 2

Lewis B. Smedes, *Forgive and Forget* (Pocket Books, 1984), 39-41

King James Version, *The Word in Life Study Bible* (Thomas Nelson Publishers, 1993), 572, 1705

II Samuel 13:1-20

Matthew 6:14; 11:25

Chapter 3

King James Version, *The Word in Life Study Bible* (Thomas Nelson Publishers, 1993), 473-483

Chapter 4

King James Version, *The Word in Life Study Bible* (Thomas Nelson Publishers, 1993), 572, 1705

(Book of Luke 13:11-13, 16)

(Book of II Corinthians 10:4-5)

(Book of Isaiah 54:17,)

(Book of Thesolonians 2:16-17)

Chapter 5

King James Version, *The Word in Life Study Bible* (Thomas Nelson Publishers, 1993), 572, 1705

Book of Luke 3:1-3

Book of Proverbs 22:6

Book of Ephesians 6:1-9;

Book of Galatians 5:19-21

Book of Romans 1:18-32

Book of Leviticus 18:1-30

II Corinthians 10:4

Psalms 19:14; 101:3

Chapter 6

King James Version, *The Word in Life Study Bible* (Thomas Nelson Publishers, 1993), 572, 1705

Book of Isaiah
Book of Romans 8:29-31;11:29
Book of St. John 3:19; 10:10
Book of Jeremiah 1:5, 29:10, 11
Book of Ephesians 4:8

Chapter 7

King James Version, *The Word in Life Study Bible* (Thomas Nelson Publishers, 1993), 572, 1705

ABOUT THE AUTHOR

Candace Cole travels throughout the U.S. touching lives in conferences, revivals, workshops, retreats and on college campuses. Her passion is found in her commitment to encourage both adult and children survivors of abuse.

Candace is an anointed vessel. Ordained by God to minister the Gospel through the arts. Candace Cole is President/Founder of CCP ("Candace Cole Theatrical Productions") as well as an acclaimed Playwright, and Producer. She is an award winning creator of theatrical musicals known throughout Southern California such as: "Busline 210, "My Child, My Child", "The Anointing", and "Where Shall My Shame Go"?

Candace is no stranger to our Los Angeles Community as the Director and CEO of The Dare To Dream Scholarship Society Incorporated, (a Non-Profit Corporation). DTDSS, is designed to assist "At Risk" students in achieving their academic and artistic goals.

Candace serves on the teaching staff at Faithful Central Bible Church ministering in the New Members Department. She also facilitates Women's Discipleship classes. She is a vessel of honor with the pen of a ready writer. Prepare your heart for the prolific writings of Author, Candace Yvette Cole.

-Danita Patterson, CEO
DESTINY UNLIMITED INC.
Media Content Developer
Chicago, IL.

HAS THIS BOOK HELPED YOUR LIFE IN ANY WAY? WE WOULD LOVE TO HEAR FROM YOU. PLEASE WRITE US AND SHARE YOUR STORY OR TESTIMONY AT THE ADDRESS BELOW:

In my opinion, the book was:
a. Good
b. Relevant
c. Edifying
d. Excellent

My favorite chapter(s) was:
Chapter 1
Chapter 2
Chapter 3
Chapter 4
Chapter 5
Chapter 6
Chapter 7

In my opinion, this book will help
A) Many women
B) Few women
C) Men and women
D) Young adults
E) Counselors
Other:____

Would you buy this book for someone you know?
A) No
B) Yes

In your opinion, would this book be good for workshops, book circles, and round table discussions?
A)Yes
B)No

Do you think this book can be used as a healing tool?
A) Yes
B) No

Were you shocked at the contents in any of the chapters you read? If your answer is yes, which ones and why?
A) Yes
B) No
C) Partly

(All comments, testimonies will be kept and may be used in future publications, media promotions; and a part of radio excerps).

If you would like to order additional copies of this book, please send your check made payable to Candace Cole in the amount of $15.00 plus $2.50 for shipping & handling.

Date:______________________________

Shipt to:____________________________
____
____

You can write to us at our e-mail address
CCPPROD@AOL.COM or click on to our website for additional info.
www.candacecole.com
Candace Cole Publications
2690 W. Imperial Hwy. #124
Inglewood, CA 90303

Please charge to my credit card:
Visa#_____________________________
Exp. Date__________________________
MasterCard#________________________
Exp. Date__________________________
Signature:__________________________
Date:_____________________________
Daytime Telephone:___________________

Upcoming new release:

Scars (A Novel Based on A True Story)

Engagements & Events

If you are interested in more information regarding speaking engagements, workshops, or theatrical productions write or call: Candace Publications at 2690 W. Imperial Hwy. Suite 124, Inglewood, CA. 90303 or Telephone us at :(310) 821-8147.

ADDITIONAL WRITINGS BY CANDACE COLE

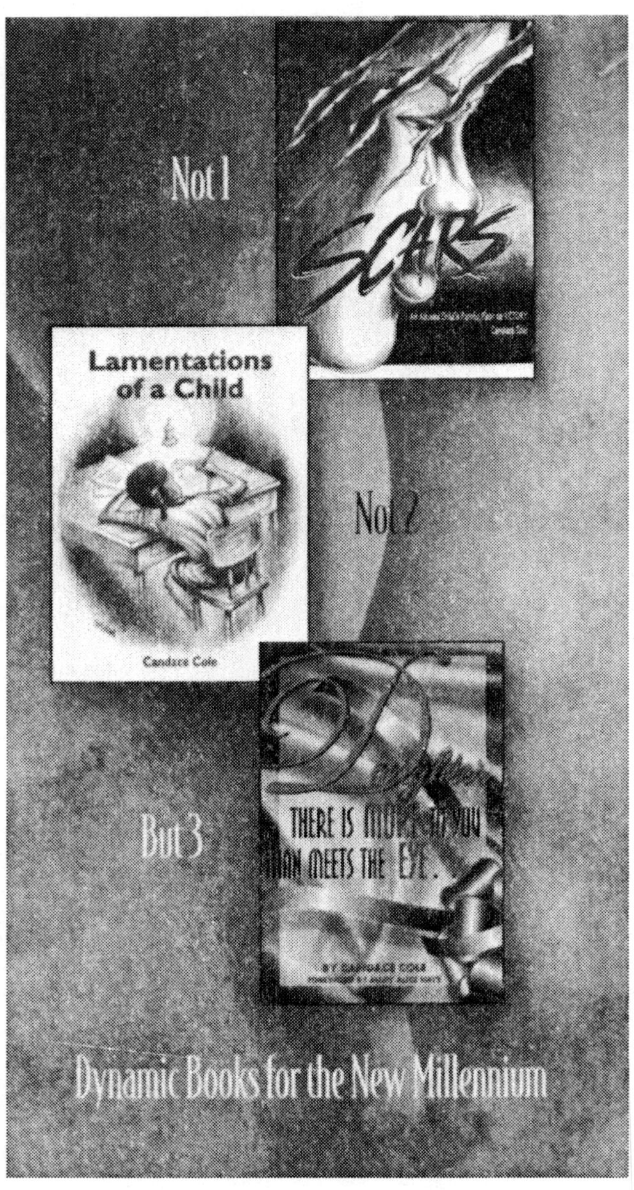